Taunton's

BUILD LIKE A PRO®
EXPERT ADVICE FROM START TO FINISH

Patios and Walkways

Patios and Walkways

Peter Jeswald

The Taunton Press

The Taunton Press
Inspiration for hands-on living®

The Taunton Press, Inc., 63 South Main Street, P.O. Box 5506, Newtown, CT 06470-5506
e-mail: tp@taunton.com

EDITOR: Jennifer Renjilian Morris

COPY EDITOR: Diane Sinitsky

JACKET/COVER DESIGN: Kimberly Adis

INTERIOR DESIGN: Kimberly Adis

LAYOUT: Cathy Cassidy

ILLUSTRATOR: Mario Ferro

PHOTOGRAPHER: Walter Goodridge, except where noted: p. 4: © The Taunton Press Inc., photo by John M. Rickard, p. 5: (top) Pavers by Ideal; (middle and bottom) © The Taunton Press Inc., photo by John M. Rickard, p. 7: (top left) © The Taunton Press Inc., photo by John M. Rickard; (top right) Pavers by Ideal; (bottom) Pavers by Ideal, p. 8: © The Taunton Press Inc., photo by John M. Rickard , p. 9: © The Taunton Press Inc., photo by John M. Rickard, p. 10: (left) © The Taunton Press Inc., photo by Jerry Bates; (right) © The Taunton Press Inc., photo by John M. Rickard, p. 11: (top left and bottom left) © The Taunton Press Inc., photo by Jerry Bates; (bottom right) © The Taunton Press Inc., photo by John M. Rickard, p. 13: Pavers by Ideal, p. 15: © The Taunton Press Inc., photo by John M. Rickard, p. 17: (top) Pavers by Ideal; (middle top) © The Taunton Press Inc., photo by John M. Rickard; (middle bottom) © The Taunton Press Inc., photo by Brian Pontolilo, courtesy *Fine Homebuilding*; (bottom) © The Taunton Press Inc., photo by Steve Silk, courtesy *Fine Gardening*, p. 18 Pavers by Ideal, p. 19 © The Taunton Press Inc., photo by John M. Rickard, p. 20 (middle) © The Taunton Press Inc., photo by Todd Meier, courtesy *Fine Gardening*; (bottom) © The Taunton Press Inc., photo by John M. Rickard, p. 22: © The Taunton Press Inc., photo by Jerry Bates, p. 23: (left) © The Taunton Press Inc., photo by Jennifer Benner, courtesy *Fine Gardening* (right) © The Taunton Press Inc., photo by Brian Pontolilo, courtesy *Fine Hombuilding*, p. 24 Pavers by Ideal, p. 25: (bottom) © The Taunton Press Inc., photo by Carl Weese, p. 26: (left) © The Taunton Press Inc., photo by Brian Pontolilo, courtesy *Fine Homebuilding*; (right) © The Taunton Press Inc., photo by John Rickard, p. 27: © The Taunton Press Inc., photo by Steve Silk, courtesy *Fine Gardening*, p. 28: © The Taunton Press Inc., photo by Brian Pontolilo, courtesy *Fine Homebuilding*, p. 35: (bottom) © The Taunton Press Inc., photo by Carl Weese, p. 37: © The Taunton Press Inc., photo by Chris Green, courtesy *Fine Homebuilding*, p. 43: (top left) © The Taunton Press Inc., photo by Chris Green, courtesy *Fine Homebuilding*, p. 52: © The Taunton Press Inc., photo by Brian Pontolilo, courtesy *Fine Homebuilding*, p. 54: Pavers by Ideal

Library of Congress Cataloging-in-Publication Data

Jeswald, Peter.
  Patios and walkways : Taunton's build like a pro : expert advice from
start to finish / Peter Jeswald.
    p. cm.
  ISBN 978-1-60085-075-2
  1. Patios--Design and construction--Amateurs' manuals. I. Title.
  TH4970.J483 2009
  690'.893--dc22

                    2009031651

Printed in the United States of America
10 9 8 7 6 5 4 3 2 1

ACKNOWLEDGMENTS

This book is a collaborative effort and would not have been possible without the help, hard work, and input of many people. I would like to thank:

My editors, Jennifer Renjilian Morris for her expertise and unflagging attention to detail, and Helen Albert for asking me to author this book and setting out such clear parameters.

Walter Goodridge, my close and multitalented friend, who provided so much more to this book than just the photography.

David Vreeland, my good friend who, once again, answered many technical questions and offered important insight.

Tim Korytoski and Justin Pelis of North Country Landscapes (pp. 56–107 and pp. 124–149), Kim Harwood of Kim Harwood Stonework (pp. 108–123), Chris and Suzanne Baxter of Whirlwind Fine Garden Design (pp. 150–167), and their talented, hardworking crews who good-naturedly put up with our frequent requests to "hold it right there" and "do that one more time?" Their professional expertise and skill made this book possible.

The owners of the projects we documented for graciously allowing Walter and me to hover around their homes like two birds of prey, swooping in when the time was right.

Landscape architects Sue Reed ("From Bland to Beautiful") and David Valbracht ("Formal Front Walkway" and "Dine in Style") for sharing their time and thinking about the projects they designed that are covered in this book.

I also thank the following people for taking time out of their busy schedules to answer my questions, share their insights, or provide much-appreciated information: Mickey Grybko, sales manager, Amherst Farmers Supply, Amherst, Massachusetts; Steve Skowyra, Lane Construction, Granby, Massachusetts; Larry Nicolai, senior vice president, and Patti Feeley, Ideal Concrete Block Company, Inc.; Ted Corvey, paver business director, Pine Hall Brick; Donna DeNinno, Dick Gruenwald Associates; Thomas L. Coffman, president, and Tamara Lytle, Coffman Stone Co.

CONTENTS

INTRODUCTION

Thirty years ago, as I revved up my chainsaw and prepared to clear our sloping house site—my wife and infant son watching from the edge of the field—I had a vision. I saw our house nestled into the south-facing hillside. A detached garage, at right angles to the house, held back the east side of the hill, carving out a path for the driveway. The house and garage, joined together by a covered walkway, cradled a stone wall-enclosed entry patio. The lawn in front of the house sloped gently to the edge of our newly created pond. What a grand vision it was; but I was patient, and slowly, over the years and with a bit of luck, that vision has been realized beyond my expectations.

Perhaps you, too, have a vision: a quiet retreat where you can unwind after a long, hard day or a new and stunning replacement to your falling-to-pieces walkway that will shepherd your guests to your front door in style. If so, you've come to the right place.

Patios and Walkways is a practical, step-by-step manual that teaches you how to build patios and walkways like a professional. Organized to help you approach your project logically and effectively, the first few chapters

get you started on the right foot and provide a valuable overview of the entire process. The first chapter explains the value of proper planning, and how to design a beautiful and functional patio or walkway. Materials are, of course, an important piece of the construction puzzle, and *Patios and Walkways* introduces the many types of materials available and explains how to choose the right one for your project. The third chapter contains a wealth of general information that applies to many of the project chapters, so you may want to refer to it as you're building.

The six project chapters describe how to construct several types of patios and walkways. From site preparation, layout, and excavation, right through to the installation of the finish materials, *Patios and Walkways* leaves nothing to chance. Even if your project is different from those presented here, you'll be able to use the basic construction techniques from each project to guide you, changing the measurements or materials as needed to add your personal touch and fit your space.

So, there's no time like the present to roll up your sleeves and get to work. And with this book as your guide, you can start your project with confidence and complete it with pride.

PLANNING AND DESIGN

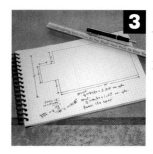
I **have a confession to make. Even though I'm** a professional designer, when it comes to doing projects around my own home, I can be a bit impatient. It's tempting to ignore advice I regularly give my clients—instead of allotting the time to think things out, I want to jump right in. Clear the ground, dig out the topsoil, move that pile of stones—I'm eager to do tasks that feel like "real" work. Well, experience and mistakes are excellent teachers, and over the years I've learned my lessons well—up-front time *is* real, and important, work.

Taking the time to adequately plan your project accomplishes several things. It helps you avoid missteps and delays; gives you the time to incorporate special features and shop for bargains; and lets you set and stay within a budget. So, I encourage you to give planning and design its due. ▶ ▶ ▶

Assess Your Needs

At the beginning of the planning process, it's important to look at the big picture first, before narrowing your focus to the specifics of your project. Gather as much information as you can. Read design and idea books and magazines, visit model homes that feature finished landscaping, and tour your local neighborhoods. The Web is, of course, an invaluable resource. You can view online portfolios, visit manufacturers' Web sites, and see projects from all over the country. Keep the clippings and photos of the projects that you like organized in a binder or folders so you can easily access them when you're ready to start.

Once you've got your information, carefully assess your situation so that you don't rush into a project and end up building something that really doesn't suit your needs. Take an inventory of your house and property. Even if you're contemplating doing a relatively small, self-contained project, it's quite likely that your house could benefit from other landscape improvements that could be considered now but constructed at another time. With a critical and, if possible, unbiased eye, note the aspects of your landscape that you do and don't like, those that do and don't work, and the features that you'd like to accentuate or hide. Afterward, take some time to brainstorm as many solutions as possible—no matter how wild or farfetched they may seem. Then, think about what you really want and need to have, choose the most viable options, and write them down in the form of a prioritized wish list (see the sidebar below).

After you've decided what project to build, it's time to develop your design.

Patio Design Basics

As you develop the design for your patio, there are several key factors to consider. Even seemingly small changes in location and orientation can improve a patio dramatically.

Location and size

Of prime importance is the location of a patio relative to the house. When possible, patios should be built near rooms that serve similar functions. This means a cooking/dining patio is best located off the kitchen or dining room, a patio intended for quiet relaxation might be adjacent to a study or bedroom, and a children's play patio could be just outside a walk-out basement.

Ease of access is another important consideration. Patios that are built next to the house should be constructed as close as possible to the height of the indoor floor level. Wide French doors that can remain open without impinging interior space are a big plus. Patios located away from the house should be linked to the house with well-defined and appropriately sized walkways.

Creating a Wish List

AT THE BEGINNING OF THE PLANNING PROCESS, it's helpful to create a wish list. Although you may not end up building, or even actually wanting, all the items you initially put on that list, going through the process encourages you to consider all the options up front. Here are some questions to help guide your list. Prioritize your list when it's done.

• What activities need to be accommodated now and in the near future?

• What practical needs do you need to address and how might those needs change as your family grows and ages?

• What aesthetic goals do you have? Are there desirable features on your property that you would like highlight?

• Is there a specific problem or issue that you'd like to resolve?

• How much money are you planning to spend on your landscaping projects?

Nestled against the soft, green foliage, the bistro table and small stone patio create the perfect place for intimate conversations.

Two furniture groupings make the most out of one corner of this patio, yet they are positioned with adequate space between them, which creates a clear path to the gate.

A low retaining wall can raise a patio to the level of the house floor, while brick siding and a roof gutter eliminate any potential problems caused by water and rain.

Another thing to keep in mind when determining the size of a patio is the furniture. Because patios are often used for large gatherings, take into account how many tables and chairs you'll need to comfortably accommodate everyone.

Sight lines and privacy

After the major decisions of location and size are made, fine-tune your patio by turning your attention to sight lines and privacy. At different places and times of day, stand or sit where the patio will be built. For example, to get a sense of what it will be like to eat on a dining patio, sit in the chosen spot in the morning, noon, and evening. Consider:

The view:
• Is there a particular view that is important to capture?
• Will you be able to keep an eye on children?

Moving the proposed location of a seating group or table may enhance the view.

Privacy:
• Will your neighbors be looking "over your shoulder" from their first- or second-floor windows?

TRADE SECRET

Size is a crucial aspect of patio design. It's a well-known phenomenon that outdoor spaces "feel" smaller than the same size interior spaces. While a 12-ft. by 16-ft. dining space might work fine indoors, it's likely to be visually inadequate as a patio. In addition, the functional space of patios that are raised off of the ground, even if just 6 in. to 12 in., is reduced considerably because people tend to stay away from the patio's edges. On the other hand, building a raised wall or installing a railing around the perimeter effectively enlarges a raised patio.

PRO TIP

There's something magical about being outside, watching and listening to the rainfall. To provide shelter for these quiet moments, consider extending the roof over a section of patio.

• Do you want seclusion from your own family?
• Is there something you'd rather not see?

Plantings, fencing, or an arbor can screen out those prying eyes or an unpleasant sight line.

Noise:
• The traffic from a nearby street
• The sound of a neighbor's TV
• Boisterous children at play

Noise doesn't like to turn corners, so you can minimize its impact by positioning a solid object, such as a building or solid fence, between you and the offending source. Introducing the "white" or "pink" noise created by fountains, artificial waterfalls, or lush choirlike music into your patio can muffle or cancel out unwanted sounds.

The elements

Whether you want them to or not, two guests—the sun and wind—will visit your patio frequently. And, depending on the time of the day, year, or part of the country in which you live, they may or may not be welcome.

• In the spring the warming effects of the sun are enjoyable.
• The hot summer sun can turn a patio into a furnace.
• Gentle, cooling breezes are welcome in summer.
• The winds in spring and fall can chill outdoor spaces.

Eastern exposures tend to warm up quickly in the morning, while unprotected western exposures can overheat in the afternoon. If possible, orient your patio to take advantage of a shady tree or make use of umbrellas or a retractable awning. When it's not practical or possible to position a patio so that the house blocks chilling winds, a strategically constructed fence may do the job.

Walkway Design Basics

To create more than merely a utilitarian means of getting from point A to point B, there are a number of design elements—including shape, size, beginnings, goals, and transitions—that you should consider.

Shape and size

When planning a walkway, the shape is typically considered first. To get an initial sense of the shape of your walkway, you can actually walk from beginning to end along the path that you take naturally. As you may discover, people tend

Types of Walkways

PERHAPS YOUR PROPERTY is in need of more than one walkway. A network of walkways and paths creates an organized yet attractive way to move people through your landscape. Walkways can be broken down into three categories based primarily on how they're used and their relative size.

PRIMARY WALKWAYS

Primary walkways are the most frequently used type of walkway. Wide enough to easily accommodate two people walking side by side, they may stand alone or have other walks branch off of them. A walk that leads to the front door is an obvious example, but a well-traveled walkway from the garage to a side door could also be considered a primary walk. Choose the material for a primary walk carefully because it should not only be attractive but also provide secure footing. Loose materials are not a good choice here as they are likely to get tracked into the house, might shift underfoot, and are difficult to clear of snow.

SECONDARY WALKWAYS

Secondary walkways may branch off of primary and other secondary walks, but they can also stand alone. Although typically narrower than primary walks, they too can be wide enough for two people to walk side by side. Often utilitarian in nature, secondary walkways might need to accommodate someone pushing a wheelbarrow from a shed to the garden or carrying a trash can from the house to the garage. The choice of material is mainly driven by how the walkway will be used. "Working" walkways must be firm underfoot, and walks that need to be cleared of snow should have smooth, solid surfaces.

TERTIARY WALKWAYS

Perhaps best described as paths, tertiary walkways are the narrowest, most informal type of walk. They might skirt discreetly around the corner of a house or lead to an out-of-the-way patio or garden. Typically they're only wide enough for one person. Given their informal nature and the numerous ways that tertiary walkways can be used, just about any walkway material is appropriate for these paths.

Narrow walks that are covered with widely spaced flagstones should be used in casual settings where speed is not important. The uneven surfaces of these stones often mean that you have to watch where you step, slowing you down but giving you time to enjoy your surroundings.

to choose the most direct route and cut corners to get where they're going. To shift the walkway, to introduce curves, or to turn right angles without making the walk feel contrived, try some of the techniques described in the following sections.

While the width of a walkway is certainly governed by how it's going to be used—people walking side by side or someone pushing a wheelbarrow—aesthetics also play a role. For example, a walk to the front door that's wide enough for two people might feel too small if

A strategically located walkway can serve double duty—providing access to the front door from both the driveway and the sidewalk. This walkway appears sculpted to fit the landscape as it curves toward the driveway entrance and then out and around a planting bed.

A low hedge is an excellent way to create a definite edge. Be sure to keep it trimmed so that it doesn't encroach too much; if you don't, you'll lose sight of the walk and, after a rain, get your pants wet for good measure.

TRADE SECRET

Use these dimensions as a guide when determining the width of your walkway:

- 12 in. to 18 in.: Single file, slow pace with attention downward, usually stepping stones
- 18 in. to 2 ft. 6 in.: Single file, quicker pace
- 2 ft. 6 in. to 4 ft.: One person carrying a trash can or pushing a wheelbarrow
- 4 ft. or wider: Two people walking abreast

it traverses a large expanse of lawn or leads to a sumptuous entrance. Of course, the converse can be true. Also, the width of a walkway does not have to remain the same. As it nears the destination, a walk might widen to embrace a set of steps or contract as it enters a flower garden.

Delineating the walk

Even after carefully laying out your walkway along a route you think is best, some people might still cut corners or leave the walk. Delineating a walkway with a clear edge or boundary will help these folks avoid temptation and stay on track. The solution might be as simple as incorporating a distinct, perhaps even raised, border. Flower beds, shrubs, and hedges create effective boundaries. Low fences and stone walls can be used in trouble spots where the pull to leave the path is particularly strong.

Beginnings, goals, and transitions

Although every walkway has a beginning, not all beginnings are created equal. Entrances don't have to be monumental, but they should be easy to identify. A clearly defined beginning provides a sense of arrival and separation between different areas. Widening the walkway at the beginning is a simple, straightforward technique. Wooden posts, stone pillars, or large rocks are excellent markers. Openings in stone walls or fences, tall columns, or pergolas create a more dramatic sense of entry.

Goals grab attention and encourage people to keep moving. Plantings, rock groupings, sculpture, and garden ornaments all make excellent goals. Use goals judiciously and locate them so that they have a sense of place and don't feel arbitrary. A good strategy is to locate the first goal close to, and within sight of, the beginning. Longer walkways can benefit from more than

Several visual cues are used here to mark the transition from stone-paver patio to walkway. Larger stones of a different color placed in the walk are the first indicators, followed by sturdy brick pillars, and finally a one-piece stone step.

Fountains can not only act as goals, catching our interest and pulling us forward, but they also enliven the journey by adding sound and a sense of movement to the experience.

one goal. For example, a 40-ft. walk might have the first goal 10 ft. from the beginning and the second goal 15 ft. from the first.

A walkway will feel more alive if transitions are clearly marked rather than letting them blend into one another. A subtle technique is to alter the installation pattern of the walkway material; to make a bolder statement, change the type of material altogether. The techniques used to mark the beginning can also be employed to mark walkway transitions.

How to Design Your Project

With the preliminaries out of the way, you can now begin to develop a design. This requires some drawing, but don't be intimidated. The drawings don't have to be works of art, and you don't need a lot of fancy drafting equipment. You can make perfectly serviceable drawings with a mechanical pencil, straightedge, and some graph paper. Developing a design requires two steps—making a site plan and creating a finished design.

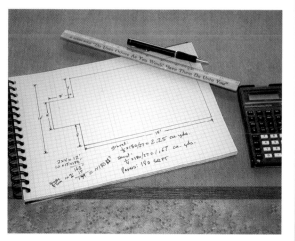

PROTIP

To help guide your lines and make drawing to scale easy, use ¼-in. graph paper, which provides a "built-in" scale of ¼ in. per foot.

You can buy graph paper in many forms—notebooks, glued pads, and large sheets. It's also available in tracing paper versions, which allows you to trace over a drawing, rather than having to re-create the second drawing totally from scratch.

Site plan

A site plan is a "map" of your property that shows the existing structures and indicates the topography, or "lay of the land." The level of detail required in a site plan is influenced by the size and complexity of the project. For limited projects, such as those covered in this book, adequate site plans can be created using tape measures and levels. More sophisticated plans might require the professional services of a surveyor, civil engineer, or landscape architect. While there's no need to document your entire property, your site plan should encompass the entire area that's going to be impacted by your project (see the illustration below).

Locate physical structures A site plan should show the location of all relevant and existing items aboveground and belowground such as:

• Your house, garage, sheds, pool, play structures, patios, decks, and walkways
• The septic system or sewer pipes, and well or water lines
• Underground utilities such as gas, electricity, and cable TV
• Topographic features of your property such as trees, rocks or ledge outcroppings, plantings, and wet areas
• The slope, or grade change, that occurs within the bounds of your project

Environmental considerations Several environmental considerations should be included on a site plan:

• The compass reading (orient the drawing in a way that feels right—usually the front door at the bottom of the drawing)
• Solar exposure
• The direction of the cooling summer breezes and nasty winter winds
• The views you'd like to capture and those you'd like to screen out

SITE PLAN

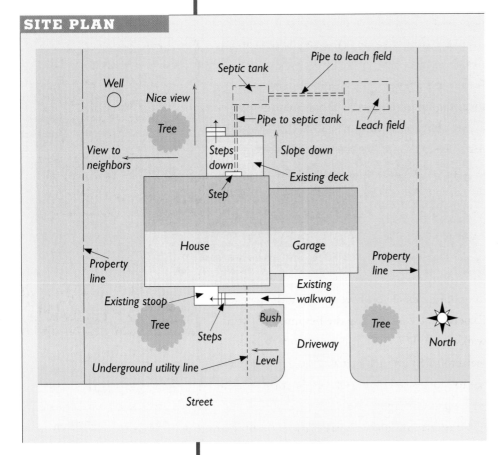

Steps are an efficient, attractive way to get from the bottom to the top of slopes and hillsides. Landings provide a place to rest and allow the steps to conform to the pitch of the hill.

Finished design

Even though you may be an amateur weekend warrior, you can approach this process much like a design professional would—work in broad strokes before attending to details, and consider several design solutions before drawing your final design to scale.

Look at the big picture first As you begin to design your patio or walkway, look at the bigger issues such as size, shape, and location before designing intricate paving patterns or planning the planting beds. If your project will include a set of stairs, indicate them on the drawing, but don't worry about the precise rise and run. That will come later.

To avoid getting hung up on the details at this stage, keep your drawings loose and rough. Tissue tracing paper is excellent for this purpose. It has an informal feel and it's cheap, so you can use lots of it.

Of course, details are important, and as your design matures and you start to work on them, you'll find that the details will influence and alter the final design.

Consider multiple designs Although it's a trap that's all too easy to fall into, don't get locked into your first design. Early in my design career, I sometimes got too attached to my initial designs. It took me a few years to really understand that investing time in multiple design solutions is critical. Even if I ended up with a final design that was similar to the first one, the exploration invariably enriched the ultimate result.

To help you do this, commit to trying out at least three different options. For example, take a square dining patio and bump out a place for a bistro table and two chairs. Or perhaps a rectangle or some other shape is better suited for that long dining table you have stored in the garage. Experiment with putting the beginning of your walkway in different locations, even if they don't seem to make any sense at all. And, if you're partial to straight lines and right angles, play around with curving shapes.

Draw the finished design Once you have decided on a final design, draw a finished, "hard line" plan. Using the lines of the graph paper as a guide, draw the plan of your project to scale. It's best to begin by drawing the large fixed objects,

PRO TIP

As you measure the existing features, transcribe the measurements on graph paper, creating a rough drawing. Do the finish drawing later.

TRADE SECRET

On your site plan, indicate any trees and bushes you want to remove and those you want to save, as well as any structures—such as existing walkways or steps—that you want demolished. If there will be a lot of "deconstruction," consider creating a separate demolition plan.

TRADE SECRET

Early designs can be rough. Place tissue tracing paper over the site plan and draw freehand. You can build on each design by overlaying additional sheets of tissue.

Privacy fence

Tree

Patio is located to be closer to tree.

Property line

Steps

Step

New patio

Width of patio

Length of patio

House

Garage

New guest parking/turnaround

Distance to walkway

New landing

Planting bed

Width of walkway at entrance

New steps

New walkway

North

Property line

New boulder

Driveway

Street

Vertical stone or post

Lighting Options

EXTERIOR LIGHTING IS AN IMPOR-
TANT PART of patio and walkway design.
Designed well, lighting can add both
safety and beauty. The same lights that
make a walkway easy to see and travel
can also create an attractive scene.

TYPES OF LIGHTING

There are three basic types of lighting to
choose from.

- Solar lighting: Solar lighting, as the name
  implies, gets its power from the sun. It
  is the easiest type of lighting to install.
  Solar fixtures can be placed anywhere
  and moved easily, and they turn themselves on after dusk without the need for
  an external timer. Although they provide
  enough light for many outdoor situations,
  they are not as bright as low- or high-
  voltage lights. But they do cost less to
  install, and they won't add to your electricity bill.

- Low-voltage lighting: Low-voltage lights
  are powered by a voltage transformer
  that is typically plugged in to a household receptacle. Individual fixtures are
  connected in a series with wiring, which
  is buried several inches under the
  ground. Fixtures can be purchased separately or as a part of a kit that includes
  the transformer, wire, fixtures, and con-
  nectors. Low-voltage lighting can be
  installed by do-it-yourselfers.

- High-voltage lighting: High-voltage
  lights use standard household current
  and usually require a dedicated circuit.
  High-voltage lighting is the most costly
  to operate and should be installed by a
  licensed professional.

TRADE SECRET

If your project covers
a large area, such as a
long walkway, it might
not fit on an 8½-in. by
11-in. sheet of paper. You
can buy larger gridded
sheets but it's easier to
use the smaller piece
of paper. One trick is to
decrease the scale of the
drawing. For example,
instead of having one
¼-in. square equal 1 ft.,
make it equal 2 ft. The
resulting ⅛-in. scale
allows you to put twice
as much on a given sheet
of paper.

such as the house and garage, and then drawing
the patio or walkway relative to them.

Work slowly and carefully, taking the time to
get the size of your patio and walkway accurate.
Include the critical dimensions, such as the overall size, length, and width, the location where
walkways begin, and the radii of any curves. You
can also make notes on the plan, communicating
important information.

After you've finished your plan, let it rest for
a while. Then come back to it and walk around
your yard, trying to envision what the finished
product will look like. It might be a good idea
to ask for some feedback from family members
and friends.

When you are satisfied, set up a construction
schedule and order your materials.

TYPES OF FIXTURES

There is virtually an endless array of lighting fixtures, but they can be broken down into several general categories.

- Spotlights: Spotlights provide a powerful, focused beam of light that is well suited to lighting up a specific object.

- Floodlights: Floods also produce a powerful beam of light. The beams are wider than spotlights, though, and are used to light up larger areas.

- Globe lights: Globe lights produce a softer, diffuse light that provides general overall lighting.

- Down lights and up lights: As their names suggest, down and up lights have shades that cast their light down or up. Their light is not as focused as spotlights and not as diffuse as globe lights.

- Specialty lights: The variety of lights intended for specific uses seems endless. Lights are built into pavers and stepping stones, or as part of statuary bases, fake rocks, and other garden elements. There are also fixtures designed to be installed in the risers of steps (see the photo above).

LIGHTING TECHNIQUES

Beautiful lighting isn't just about the fixtures. You can choose from several techniques to enhance the natural beauty of your patio, walkway, or their surroundings.

- Shadowing: Use this technique to highlight interesting shapes, like a large plant or the branch structure of a tree. Place the light source in front of the object and aim it so that a shadow is cast on a surface such as a wall or board fence.

- Silhouetting: Use this technique to outline and emphasize the shape of an object like a tree or piece of sculpture. Place the light source behind the object and shine the light against a solid surface like a wall or fence.

- Moon lighting: To achieve this effect, place the light source up in a tree and shine the light down through the branches. The resulting shadows will make it appear that the moon is shining.

MATERIALS

Successfully transforming the plans for your patio or walkway into reality requires knowledge of the available building materials. In addition to carefully reading the information provided here, I encourage you to take a few trips to get some hands-on experience. Stop by local material suppliers. Pick up a brick or concrete paver. Run your hand across the top to get a sense of the surface texture. Note the color differences in the various types of stone. If there's a gravel pit or stone quarry near you, visit it to get a better sense of production methods. Here, familiarity breeds respect and an appreciation of the materials you will use.

One lesson that most professionals learn early in their careers, and that you'd be wise to heed, is "don't try to do it on the cheap." Money spent on the appropriate materials is a wise investment–they will look good from the start and age gracefully. ▶ ▶ ▶

Choose the Right Materials

Some of the materials used to build patios and walkways are as old as the hills and have been used for centuries. Others are new materials made possible by modern manufacturing techniques and sometimes produced in response to growing environmental concerns. Choosing the appropriate materials for your project is a bit like conducting a symphony. You have to orchestrate the right balance of aesthetic and functional considerations.

Obviously you want your patio or walkway to be aesthetically pleasing, but beauty doesn't just happen. It takes a little effort. The choice of material should fit the style of your home and landscape. The uniform profile of cut stone suggests formality, while irregularly shaped flagstones have an informal quality. The installation

Perhaps the simplest of all paver installation patterns is the running bond, and it's clear from this photo how it earned its name. Oriented in the direction of travel, this walkway, edged with a soldier-course border, fairly sweeps you toward the gate.

pattern can reinforce a desired effect. An intricate herringbone pattern adds to a formal feel, while a simple running bond is more informal. Color choice is also important. Rich, strong colors that contrast with the color of a house make a strong statement, while softer, muted colors tend to blend into the landscape.

In addition to being beautiful, materials need to fit their function. For example, rough-faced stone flagging with wide joints is not the best choice for a dining patio, where stable footing for the table and chairs is important. Loose-fill materials, such as pea stone or bark mulch, are not the best option for a formal walk to your front door. Those materials can get stuck in shoes and tracked into the house. For situations that call for sure footing, the smooth surface of brick or concrete pavers is more appropriate than stepping stones.

Installed outdoors, all building materials will show the effects of time and the elements. Whereas some materials may deteriorate relatively quickly, others age gracefully and develop

Set at 90 degrees to the direction of travel and the fieldstone retaining wall, this herringbone pattern fits perfectly with its surroundings. The interspersed color variations of the concrete pavers echo that of the stones, adding to the effect.

a pleasing patina. Freeze/thaw cycles can wreak havoc with bricks that were not intended to be used as pavers and on mortar joints. Choose materials that work with your climate and install them properly so they'll last.

Stone

Stone is an ancient building material that has, not surprisingly, a timeless quality. And, depending on how it's shaped and finished, it is appropriate to use in rustic, casual, or formal settings. It is sold in "rough" form as it was produced at the quarry or in "dressed" or cut shapes. Stone is widely available and commonly used for building patios and walkways. As a general rule, stone that has been dressed costs more than stone that's used just as it came out of the quarry.

Stone is known by many names, such as *patio stone, flagstone,* and *flagging.* These terms can be ambiguous and confusing. Here are some of the most-used terms and what stones fall into those categories.

Irregular flagging laid with wide joints has an informal quality. In shady areas, moss makes for a vivid, low-maintenance way to visually tie the stones together. Moss doesn't have to be mowed like grass.

Stone Types

Type of Stone	Weight	Workability	Strength	Uses
Granite	Heavy	Difficult	High	Used for segmental pavers and steps, usually ordered to size
Sandstone, including bluestone	Medium	Medium to difficult	Medium	Used for flagging, segmental pavers, and treads, available in various colors
Limestone	Heavy	Medium to difficult	Medium to high	Used for flagging and wall stone
Slate	Medium	Easy	Low	Used for flagging but can be slippery
Schist	Heavy	Easy	Medium	Used for flagging, wall stone, and steps

- Flagging or flagstone pavers—These relatively large pieces of flat stone are often referred to as patio stone, but they are also used to construct walkways. Irregular flagging is a more natural-looking stone with rough, irregular sides. Typically 1 in. to 4 in. thick, it varies in size and shape. Regular, or cut, flagging has been sawn to uniform sizes, shapes, and thick-nesses, usually ranging in size from 6-in. to 3-ft. squares and rectangles and in thicknesses from 1 in. to 2 in. Schist is commonly used for irregular flagging, while sandstone (such as bluestone), limestone, and slate come in both forms.

- Wall stone—As the name suggests, wall stone is used to construct stone walls. The size and shape of wall stone varies widely and includes small, thin pieces as well as large, thick pieces. Wall stone typically has two relatively flat sides, which makes it easier to build with, but it often has to be trimmed, or even split, by hand. You can buy wall stone from a supply yard, where it is usually sold by the pallet, or directly from a stone quarry and have it deliv-ered loose in a dump truck. Schist, sandstone, and limestone are some of the stones sold as wall stone.

- Segmental stone pavers—Segmental stone pavers are smaller than flagging, although some manufacturers also refer to those large pieces as pavers. They come in a variety of shapes and sizes. The cobblestone is probably the most familiar type of stone paver, but its rough surface makes walking a little difficult. You can find stone pavers with smooth sur-faces made from granite, travertine, and blue-stone, among others.

- Fieldstone, river stone, and boulders— These stones vary depending on the region.

Fieldstone is typically more rounded than wall stone, and river stone has been rounded by the action of water, which makes them more difficult to build with. These stones are better used as a visual accent in a wall. Boulders are large, round-shaped rocks that can often be purchased from a gravel pit or stone quarry. They too can be incorporated into walls or along the sides of walkways.

• Washed stone—Produced in gravel pits, these small, rounded stones have been washed with water to remove sand and soil. They are separated and sold according to size, from $3/8$-in. pea stone up to 3 in. Washed stone is sometimes sorted for color. Use it for walks and patios or to fill the joints between flagging or pavers and for drainage.

Utility Stone and Its Uses

Name	Description	Uses
Gravel (generic)	Any sandy material that contains a mix of sand and small stones	Good draining and backfill material
Bank run gravel	Gravel straight from the gravel pit	May not be suitable for use in patios, walkways, or walls if it contains large stones
Screened gravel	Gravel that's been put through a screen to remove designated sizes	Good base material
Processed gravel	Gravel in which the stones have been crushed to a more uniform size	Excellent base material
Trap rock	Dark-colored igneous rocks, such as basalt, that have been crushed, washed, and sized	Good for wall base and drainage
Trap-rock gravel	Trap rock that includes small pieces and fines	Excellent for base and drainage material
Stone dust	Fine product produced from crushing rock	Excellent for setting beds and to fill joints in stone flagging
Crusher run stone or rock	Washed stone that has been crushed and sold with fines	Excellent base material
Crushed stone	Stone that has been crushed, screened, and washed	Excellent drainage material
Sand, generic	Loose, granular material composed of small particles of rock	Can be used to fill joints in stone flagging
Concrete sand	Fine, screened, and washed sand	Excellent and recommended for use as setting beds and joint filler for concrete pavers
Mason's or masonry sand	Finer than concrete sand	Used for mortar, not recommended for setting beds or filling joints

Estimating Materials

ESTIMATING MATERIALS REQUIRES some mathematical calculation using the concepts of square footage, cubic footage (or cubic yardage), and tons. Square footage is determined by multiplying length by width: 10 ft. x 10 ft. = 100 sq. ft. Multiply the square footage number by the thickness to get cubic footage: 100 sq. ft. x 2 ft. = 200 cu. ft. (For patios and walkways, the thickness number is a portion of a foot, for example 3 in. = 0.25 ft., 4 in. = 0.3 ft., and 6 in. = 0.5 ft.) To find cubic yardage, divide the cubic footage by 27.

Many materials that are estimated in cubic yards are actually purchased by the ton, so you have to convert your measurement into tons by multiplying the cubic yards by a conversion factor. For example, if a cubic yard of washed stone equals 1.5 tons, multiply the total yardage by 1.5 to get the total tonnage. Conversion factors vary for the specific type of sand, gravel, and stone, and, for sand and gravel, the moisture content. When ordering these materials, be sure to tell the supplier how you arrived at your figures and what conversion factor to use.

You can usually order irregular flagging, which varies in thickness, by the square foot. Larger pieces are generally more expensive than smaller ones. Regular flagging and stone, concrete, and brick pavers are also ordered by the square foot, but the amount needed varies with the pattern and shape of the patio or walkway. For example, you'll need more material for curves than for rectangular shapes. Suppliers typically have charts detailing how to order their products, and suppliers are always eager to help.

You can have some fun playing with concrete pavers of different colors. Here, where it crosses a neutral-tone driveway, the red pavers show exactly where to cross, assuring that you're on the right path.

It's comfortable dressed up with formal patterns, or at home in less formal installations that feature haphazard, fanciful designs and insets of tile or stone.

Segmental pavers have a number of advantages for do-it-yourselfers. First, their relatively small size and regular shape make them easy to handle and install. They have fairly uniform characteristics and are more predictable to work with than stone. When dry-laid (installed without mortar joints), it's easy to make changes and repairs to the finished patio or walkway. Matching color from batch to batch can be difficult, so it is a good idea to order extra pavers and store them for future use.

• Specialty stones—Stone is cut and shaped into a number of specialty items such as stair treads, one-piece steps, and benches. Each is sized according to its use. These items come in sandstones, granite, slate, and schist.

Masonry

Masonry is man's oldest manufactured building product and has been used in construction for centuries. When it comes to building modern patios and walkways, the most popular type of masonry is the ubiquitous segmental paver. Although sometimes referred to as paving *brick*, this term is misleading because segmental pavers are also made from concrete and stone. The standard 4-in. by 8-in. paver is surprisingly versatile.

Brick

Modern brick is made by heating, or firing, shale and clay to about 2000° F, which fuses the particles together to form a permanent bond. As a result, the color is integral throughout the material and will not fade over time. Different types of clay, additives, coatings, and forming methods

Although bricks made today are certainly a modern material, they somehow still manage to exude an old-world quality. Their warm, rich color goes well with the greens of lawns and gardens.

Paving bricks come with chamfered edges, which are less likely to chip or break and tend to help hide the subtle variations in height that are an inevitable part of every paver installation.

TRADE SECRET

Because recycled bricks are so attractive, it may be tempting to use them to construct your patio or walkway. But most recycled bricks are wall bricks, so they are not intended for ground-contact use. In harsh climates, the freeze/thaw cycles or deicing salts may break down the bricks over time. It's best to check with a local supply yard or mason to determine if the bricks you want to use are suitable for the job.

allow manufacturers to produce brick in a broad range of colors and textures.

Paving brick is intended for outdoor use on horizontal surfaces. Formed by either an extrusion or a molding process, paving brick has high compressive strength (resistance to crushing) and is formulated to resist water absorption and the effects of salt, chemicals, and freeze/thaw cycles.

In the past, clay pavers shrank about 10 percent during the firing process, which caused troublesome size inconsistencies among batches. Today, however, most manufacturers produce clay pavers with minimal size variations.

Although brick pavers are available in other shapes, most are rectangles. There are two general types: bonded and modular. *Bonded* brick pavers

Casting your own concrete pavers can be appealing. However, unlike precast pavers, which are formulated and manufactured to stand up to the elements, cast-in-place concrete breaks down more quickly. Instead of casting enough pavers for a small walkway or patio, try custom making a few accent pieces.

are a full 4 in. by 8 in. and are meant for mortarless installations. *Modular* brick pavers measure 3⅝ in. by 7⅝ in. and are used for mortared installations with ⅜-in. joints. Both are available in either 2¼-in. or 1⅜-in. thicknesses.

Some newer bonded pavers are made with spacer nibs, which simplify the installation. Weathered or beveled edges simulate age and eliminate the chipping that can occur with square-edge pavers.

Concrete

Concrete—a carefully measured mixture of cement, aggregate (typically washed stone), various additives, and water—is an amazingly pliant material. Poured on site or precast in a factory, concrete can be formed, molded, etched, stamped, embedded, and colored to achieve a countless number of effects. Large poured-in-place concrete jobs are more complicated than

they appear and are typically best left to professionals. On the other hand, precast concrete segmental pavers, like their brick cousins, are do-it-yourself friendly.

Manufactured under high pressure and with carefully controlled ingredients, precast concrete pavers are formulated to resist breakage, freeze/thaw cycles, and deicing salts. Concrete pavers are available in a wide array of styles and colors that mimic stone and brick, but over time the surface of the paver can wear away, exposing the underlying aggregate, making it appear that the paver has faded. Concrete pavers are manufactured with spacing nibs to facilitate installation. Some manufacturers offer exposed-aggregate pavers and pieces that are large enough to be used as stepping stones. Concrete stair treads and blocks for constructing walls are also available (see the top photo on p. 26).

Concrete pavers, wall and stair blocks, and treads can be purchased in the same style and color for a coordinated look or mixed and matched to add a little spice.

Delivery Please

STONE, BRICK, AND CONCRETE are heavy and, particularly in the quantities it takes to build the typical patio or walkway, are difficult to transport. You might be tempted to save delivery costs by picking up the materials yourself, but that is often impractical.

While it's possible to load materials such as gravel and sand by hand and transport them in a pickup truck, it's a time- and labor-intensive endeavor. Having it trucked to your site in a dump truck makes more sense. That's also true of materials sold by the pallet, like concrete and brick pavers. Loading pavers one by one is time consuming and you run the risk of breaking them. Most delivery trucks are equipped with a boom that can quickly and safely off-load entire pallets.

Unless you have extreme space limitations, it's best to have all the materials delivered at one time. This reduces the transportation costs and the chances that one delivery batch will differ from the next. This is particularly important with concrete pavers, which can vary in color from pallet to pallet. Of course, picking a few additional pieces or small quantities can be done by hand.

Whether your materials are delivered or you pick them up, it's important to plan ahead and clear a relatively level area, typically adjacent to the driveway, where they can be off-loaded. Loads of loose material like sand and gravel will spread out and need at least an 8-ft. by 8-ft. space. Pallets are typically about 3 ft. to 4 ft. square.

Bulk materials such as gravel, washed stone, and irregular flagging are typically transported to the site by dump truck. Plan ahead and have a large enough spot picked out and cleared before the truck arrives.

Pallets of concrete and brick pavers are heavy and can be difficult to move over soft ground intact. Once they are off-loaded, it's usually best to leave the pallet in place and transport the individual pavers to the work site with a wheelbarrow or hand truck.

Unless you are working with them right next to where they are delivered, you need to transport your materials to the construction site. A piece of machinery, such as a skid steer or Bobcat® equipped with a buck or a set of forks, can make quick work of this task. You can move them by hand with a wheelbarrow or hand truck. To protect an existing lawn from being damaged, lay sheets of plywood over the grass.

Modern concrete and brick pavers are designed so that when the joints between pavers are filled with sand and the pavers are compacted the sand locks the pavers together. This interlocking effect creates a uniform, stable surface.

Most paver manufacturers also produce concrete blocks intended to build block, or "segmental," walls and steps. Wall blocks are typically held together with pins or by tongue and grooves cast into the blocks. Larger blocks may be made with holes to save material and make them lighter.

Concrete paver manufacturers make pavers in myriad shapes and sizes; so many, in fact, that with a little imagination, you could create a concrete paver mosaic.

Other Options

Loose-fill and fibrous materials, such as pine needles, mulch, and wood chips, are appropriate for informal walkways and garden paths. They are soft to walk on and, when wet, can give off a pleasant, woodsy smell.

Pine needles and pine straw mulch are gaining widespread popularity. If you are lucky enough to have access to pine trees, you might be able to gather the needles yourself; if not, it is available in baled form from landscape-supply companies. Pine needles contain nutrients that are important for tree growth, so fertilize trees if you harvest frequently.

Mulch can be made from a variety of materials and comes in several forms. Bark mulch, perhaps the most common type of shredded mulch, should contain at least 85 percent of bark from the named tree. A generic mulch material may contain 70 percent of the named material, either bark or wood. The balance of the material is typically wood.

Bark nuggets are chunks of bark that has been removed from mature trees, processed to remove sticks, and graded according to size. Generally speaking, wood mulches decompose more quickly than bark mulches.

Nothing seems more in tune with the nature of a woodland path than the springy feel and visual softness of bark mulch or pine needles.

Wood chips are made from low-quality or waste wood that has been put through a knife chopper or wood chipper. Standard wood chips, sometimes referred to as "quarters," are about the size of a quarter. It's best not to get wood chips from pine trees or other species with resinous, sticky sap.

Shredded and small-particle mulches are easier to walk on and tend to knit together and stay in place better than large nuggets and chips. Mulches and chips can be purchased directly from some sawmills and landscaping suppliers.

Wood and Composites

COMPARED WITH STONE AND MASONRY, wood is relatively easy to work with. The advantage does come with a built-in disadvantage though. When used in outdoor applications, wood is not as durable as stone and masonry. Building with rot-resistant varieties or chemically treated wood helps, but it only delays the inevitable. Before choosing wood as a building material, weigh the pros and cons carefully.

In response to the burgeoning interest in low-maintenance products, recycling, and concerns about the safety of some pressure-treated products, the use and availability of composite lumber for landscaping and other outdoor applications has increased dramatically. Although some of these products are made exclusively with plastic, the majority are actually plastic composites, which are made by combining plastic resins with other materials, such as wood fibers, to reduce cost and improve performance.

Wood and composite timbers can be used for retaining walls and on-grade stairs and boards for walkway edgings.

CONSTRUCTION METHODS

1 Patios and
Walkways
p. 30

2 Walls
p. 44

3 Steps
p. 51

While each project in the following chapters is carefully and thoroughly explained, it's likely that your particular situation–the relationship of your house to the land, soil type, or regional location, for instance–will vary, at least somewhat, from those projects. Or perhaps you'd like to use a material or choose an installation pattern that's different from the ones you see in the photos. That's where this chapter comes in. It provides you with general information and alternative approaches and details so that you can make changes and modifications that suit your needs and taste.

Walls and steps are often an integral part of patios and walkways. You'll find general construction information on those topics as well so that you can incorporate them into your project. ▶ ▶ ▶

TRADE SECRET

If you decide not to remove a plant that's near the construction area, you should take some extra precautions to protect it. To keep activity away from the plant, you can install some stakes around the perimeter of the plant and tie plastic flagging tape to the stakes. Be sure to determine the extent of the root system and place the stakes outside of it. If you are going to be doing a lot of cutting near a plant, cover it with a tarp to prevent the dust from collecting on the leaves or wash off the plant with a hose after you've finished cutting.

Patios and Walkways

Although the specifics will vary from project to project, generally patios and walkways are composed of three basic components—base, setting bed, finished surface—and all usually follow the same basic six-step construction sequence. Understanding that step-by-step process will help you plan the work and complete your project in an orderly manner.

Preparing the site

Before construction can begin, the site has to be cleared of everything that is not going to be part of the finished project and of things that will be in the way during construction. This may include trees, bushes, plantings, and surface rocks. With your plan as a guide, roughly locate the overall work area and mark it with stakes. Be sure to mark out enough space to work comfortably and allow access for any large tools or equipment. It's helpful to tag or mark all that is going to be removed or saved, such as that prized bush you want to replant, particularly if you're not going to be doing all the work yourself.

Preparing the site may also entail removing an existing walkway or set of steps. Without a little "destructive investigation," there's no way to know how something is constructed or how hard it will be to demolish. Sometimes you might need a jackhammer, particularly when something is made from poured concrete.

Before you do any digging, you need to account for underground utilities. Call the Dig Safe service in your area and they will locate and mark them out.

Making an initial layout

After the site is cleared, do an initial layout of your project. This layout determines the area to

Concrete sidewalks can usually be demolished with the aid of an 8-lb. sledgehammer and some muscle.

be excavated and filled with the base material, so the measurements don't have to be extremely accurate. The final layout will be done after the site is excavated and the base prepped.

Locate reference points The most important part of the initial layout is establishing one or more reference points—for example, a corner of the house, the center of a door, the intersection of two measurements, or a specified distance away from a fixed point, such as a wall. Reference points not only provide a place to begin the layout, but they also let you reestablish locations and verify dimensions during the excavation and final layout steps.

Lay out the patio/walkway Once you have established the reference points, locate and lay out your patio or walkway. To mark rectangular shapes and straight walkways, you can use stakes and strings (see the sidebar "Creating Right Angles" on p. 40).

Free-form curves are easier to lay out with the aid of a hose. Position the hose on the ground and adjust it until it forms the shape you want.

Planning Ahead

UNLESS YOUR PROJECT IS SMALL, IT WILL PROBABLY TAKE YOU more than one day to complete. And if you can work on your project only during weekends, your project could stretch out over a month or two. Fortunately, there are some measures you can take to minimize the negative impacts that long periods of inactivity can have.

• Materials such as processed gravel, stone dust, and concrete sand are easier to work with when they contain the proper amount of moisture. To prevent your piles from drying out, getting too wet from rain, or being contaminated with twigs, leaves, and neighborhood pets, cover them with a tarp and securely weight them down.

• After a uniform-thickness setting bed has been installed, it's essential that it's not disturbed by the little feet of children or pets or compacted or eroded by rainfall. To prevent this, do not put down more setting bed than you can cover with pavers before you stop working for the day.

• With their years of experience, pros have learned to gauge how much work they can get done in a day. They know how many square feet of pavers they can install per hour and, therefore, how much setting bed to prepare at one time. Until you learn how fast you work, err on the side of caution. To start, prepare a small area, perhaps a 10 x 10 sq. ft. section of setting bed. Then, keep track of how long it takes you to cover it with pavers and match the next section of setting bed to accommodate your speed and the amount of time you have.

• Even with the best planning, you may occasionally miscalculate or get interrupted and install more setting bed than you can cover in one work session. If that happens, cover the setting bed with a large tarp or piece of polyethylene. To minimize disturbance to the sand, don't lay the tarp directly on the bed. Instead lay a series of several long 2x4s across the bed. Set one end on the installed pavers and the other on pavers placed on the ground, beyond the edge of the setting bed. Carefully spread the tarp over the 2x4s and hold it down with pavers.

• If your setting bed does get disturbed or compacted, use a rake to "fluff" up the setting bed and then rescreed.

• If you have to stop after you've laid a section of pavers but not filled in the joints, and a heavy rain is forecast, cover the pavers with a tarp. This will prevent the rain from prematurely compacting the sand between the joints and washing it out from the edges.

To reestablish a reference point, return to the locations from which you originally measured, pull two tapes out, and cross them at the correct distances.

You can then paint the outline of the hose to represent the edge of the patio or walkway. To mark the other side of a walkway, lay the hose parallel to the first line, measure out the width of the path, and paint the second line. Sometimes you can lay out a curve by eye. Using marking paint, make a series of dots that approximate the shape of the curve, then connect the dots to create a solid line outlining the desired form.

Keep in mind that the base of your patio or walkway, and therefore the excavated area, will typically be about 1 ft. wider (6 in. on each side) than the finished surface. To account for this and to guide the digging, mark this wider area with either stakes or painted lines.

TRADE SECRET

When building a rectangular patio or straight walkway with pavers, you can eliminate most of the cutting by adjusting the size of the patio or walk to the size of the pavers. Mock up a section of pavers and base the dimensions on that. For example, instead of 4 ft., a walkway might be 4 ft. 4 in. wide.

Establishing heights

The finished heights of patio and walkway surfaces are generally influenced by two factors—the height of a home's first floor relative to the adjacent ground and the topography of the surrounding landscape. Walkways typically follow the existing slopes; patios are often built as close as possible to the first floor, so they are sometimes raised above the ground.

Patio height You will encounter one of two situations when building a patio next to a house: The desired height of the patio will either be below the house siding or above it (see the drawings on the facing page). To build patios and large landings that are just one step below the first floor and would cover the siding, special precautions need to be taken to avoid potential water and rot problems with the siding.

Walkway height The height of walkways that follow the existing ground is set by the adjacent grade. However, after the walkway base has been excavated, it can sometimes be difficult to reestablish the grade height at the walkway. You can, of course, use a builder's level, but you can also use stakes and a string. At any point along the excavated walkway where you would like to find the height of the existing grade, install a pair of stakes in undisturbed ground on opposite sides of the walkway. Then measure up from ground the same distance on each stake and high enough to

CROSS-SECTION OF PAVER INSTALLATION

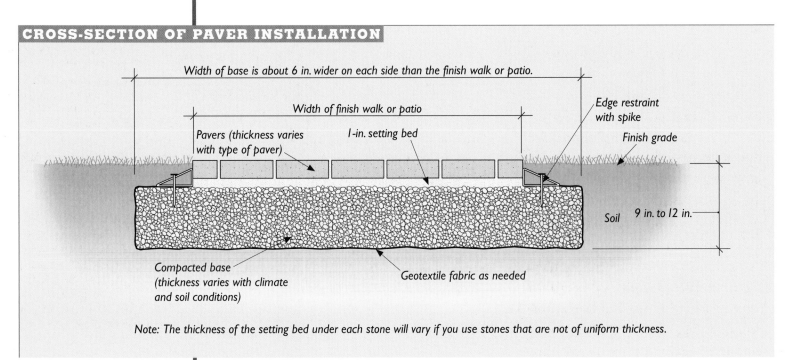

Width of base is about 6 in. wider on each side than the finish walk or patio.

Width of finish walk or patio

Edge restraint with spike

Finish grade

Pavers (thickness varies with type of paver)

1-in. setting bed

Soil 9 in. to 12 in.

Compacted base (thickness varies with climate and soil conditions)

Geotextile fabric as needed

Note: The thickness of the setting bed under each stone will vary if you use stones that are not of uniform thickness.

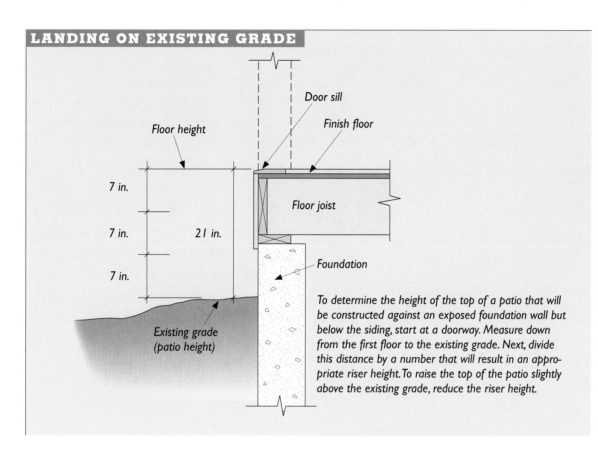

Door sill

Finish floor

Floor height

7 in.

7 in.   21 in.

7 in.

Floor joist

Foundation

Existing grade
(patio height)

To determine the height of the top of a patio that will be constructed against an exposed foundation wall but below the siding, start at a doorway. Measure down from the first floor to the existing grade. Next, divide this distance by a number that will result in an appropriate riser height. To raise the top of the patio slightly above the existing grade, reduce the riser height.

TRADE SECRET

Even if the ground on either side of a walkway is level, you can still pitch the walkway surface. Over the width of a typical 4-ft.-wide walkway, the amount of pitch will be 1 in. for a 2 percent pitch. To create the pitch, raise one edge of the walkway above the ground 1 in.; keep the other flush. Add just a little more soil against the high side and taper it toward the flush side.

---

be above any excavated material. Draw a string between the two stakes. You can measure down from the string to find the existing grade height in the walkway.

Pitch Another important consideration is pitch. To shed water and avoid potential leakage problems, patios and landings adjacent to a house should pitch away from the house. The pitch must be sufficient enough for the water to flow in the desired direction but not so steep that it is very noticeable. Generally, the pitch should be from 1 percent to 2 percent, or ⅛ in. to ¼ in., per foot. Smoother surfaces, such as concrete pavers, need less pitch than rougher ones, such as unfinished stone.

Walkways should also pitch to shed water. Walkways that are relatively level along their length should pitch across their width to prevent sheet runoff. Like patios and landings, walkways should pitch between 1 percent and 2 percent

LANDING ABOVE FOUNDATION HEIGHT

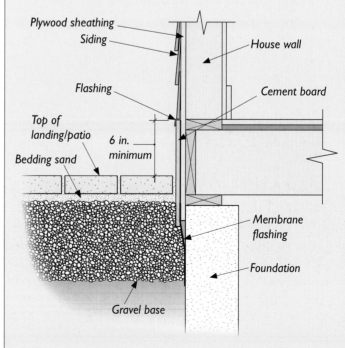

Plywood sheathing

Siding

House wall

Flashing

Cement board

Top of landing/patio

6 in. minimum

Bedding sand

Membrane flashing

Foundation

Gravel base

1. Remove the siding at the patio or landing area to at least 6 in. above where the finished surface will be.

2. Install a membrane flashing material, such as EPDM, tucking it up under the bottom course of siding and extending it down to the existing grade.

3. Slide the drip cap flashing under the siding and over the membrane.

4. Install a piece of cement board or other rot-resistant material over the existing plywood sheathing, butting it up against the drip cap flashing and extending it about ½ in. to 1 in. below the sheathing.

You can measure the desired pitch with a tape measure or put a piece of wood of the appropriate thickness —1 in. for ¼ in./ft.— under the end of a 4-ft. level.

PITCH

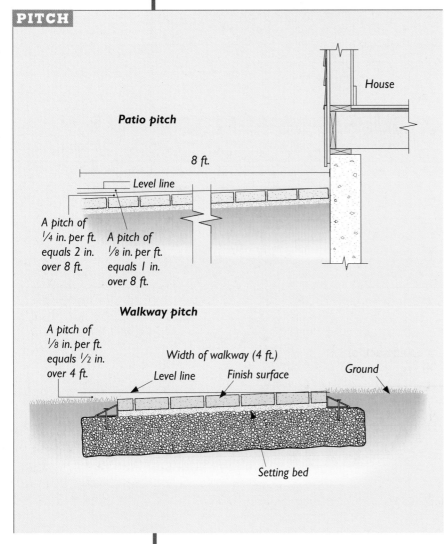

Patio pitch

House

8 ft.

Level line

A pitch of ¼ in. per ft. equals 2 in. over 8 ft.

A pitch of ⅛ in. per ft. equals 1 in. over 8 ft.

Walkway pitch

A pitch of ⅛ in. per ft. equals ½ in. over 4 ft.

Level line

Width of walkway (4 ft.)

Finish surface

Ground

Setting bed

per foot, depending on the surface material (see the drawing at left). Most walkways from the driveway naturally slope up toward the house, creating a de facto pitch.

Excavating for the base

After the site has been cleared, the base area is excavated. Excavation can be done by hand, but depending on the size of the project and the soil conditions, it can be a good investment to rent a piece of excavating equipment or hire an excavating contractor to do the work.

The exact depth of the excavation, as well as the thickness of the base, varies with climate and soil type. As a general rule, the excavation should be from 9 in. to 12 in. deep. In areas of the country that don't freeze, 9 in. is usually sufficient for well-draining soils; poor-draining or wet soils require 12 in. If you will be building on heavy clay or earth that contains a lot of organic material, consult a local professional to see how they handle these conditions.

If your soil is very moist, it's a good idea to put a layer of geotextile filter fabric in the excavated area before installing the base. This fabric

Using a Builder's Level

UNDER MOST CIRCUMSTANCES, finding height differences and establishing grades can be done using a standard 4-ft. level or a line level and string. Sometimes, though, when long distances or large changes in elevation are involved, a builder's level makes the task much easier. A builder's level is a sight level that is secured to a base, which in turn is mounted on a set of tripod legs.

To use a builder's level, first choose a spot with a clear line of sight of what you intend to measure and where the builder's level will be higher than the highest point you will measure. Then set up and adjust the level so that it is

level in all directions. Next, have a helper place a folding wooden rule or survey rod at the first location, look through the builder's level, and record the number that shows up at the level's cross hairs. If you are measuring a slope, you would first measure at the top of the slope, then at the bottom of the slope. To get your measurement, deduct the first (or smaller) dimension from the second (or larger) to get the difference in height. For example, if the top of the slope read 3 ft. 6 in. and the bottom read 7 ft. 8 in., the height difference is 4 ft. 2 in.

If you're working alone, you will need to find a way to stand the survey rod by itself.

Renting Tools

MANY OF THE TOOLS YOU'LL USE to build patios and walkways are relatively inexpensive and are useful for other projects around your house. However, there are some that are expensive or that you may use only once. It makes sense either to rent or borrow these tools.

- Electric pavement breaker (jackhammer)—Less powerful but much quieter than its air-powered cousins, an electric pavement breaker can make relatively quick work demolishing concrete walkways, patios, and steps.

- Skid steer or other small loader—This piece of equipment reduces the time and effort it takes to excavate and prep the site for patios and walkways. It can be used to remove topsoil and move and distribute sand, gravel, and rocks. When outfitted with a set of forks, the skid steer can remove pallets of building materials from delivery trucks and move them around the site.

- Plate compactor—This is an essential piece of equipment for building patios and walkways. It's used to compact soil and other materials such as crushed and trap-rock gravel.

- Handheld cut-off saw—When equipped with the proper diamond blade, this gas-powered saw can be used to cut concrete and stone.

- Brick-and-block saw—Although not as versatile as a cut-off saw, this stationary saw cuts brick, concrete, and stone pavers more accurately and safely.

This gas-powered cut-off saw is equipped with a diamond blade and is perfect for cutting stone and masonry.

- Guillotine cutter—This hand-operated cutter comes in two sizes—one for pavers and the other for blocks. It can be used to cut brick and concrete. It's safe to use, but the cuts are rougher and not as accurate as those obtained with a cut-off or brick-and-block saw.

Dealing with Excess Surface Water

EVEN IF A WALKWAY IS PITCHED PROPERLY, under certain conditions excess surface water can wash over, or puddle on top, of the walkway. If you have noticed water flooding or collecting around the area where you plan to build your walkway during heavy rains or certain times of the year, you should address this issue during the excavation phase of your project. Here's how to do it.

• Gutters—Sometimes excess surface water is a result of one or more gutter downspouts discharging large amounts of water in a concentrated area. Often the solution is quite easy: Simply change the orientation of the downspout to redirect the water flow. You may need to add a length of pipe to the downspout to carry the water to a different location. Or check if it's possible to close off the offending downspout and move it to some other section of the gutter. If none of these options will work, try one of the solutions below.

• Land form—If a walkway runs along the toe, or bottom, of a moderate or steep slope, water flowing down the hill can wash over the walkway. One way to address this situation is to change the shape of the land to create a drainage swale near the bottom of, and parallel to, the slope. The swale doesn't have to be deep, and it can be planted with grass or "disguised" by turning it into a planting bed.

• "Stone pipe"—Another way to deal with water flowing off a slope is to create a "stone pipe" along the side of the walkway that's impacted by the water (see the drawing below). When excavating the base, dig the appropriate side about 12 in. to 18 in. wider than necessary. When you install the base, cover this extra portion of the excavation with geotextile fabric and then add $1/2$-in. to $3/4$-in. washed stone up to the level of the base. Top it off with a free-draining loam and plant it, or, for added insurance, finish filling it with $3/8$-in. to $1/2$-in. washed stone.

• Low spots—The problem with low spots is that there is just no place for the water to go, and if the soil doesn't drain well or if the ground is frozen, excess water just sits on top of the ground. To fix the problem, you can dig out the poor-draining material and replace it with soil that drains well, but a more effective solution may be to fill in the low spot.

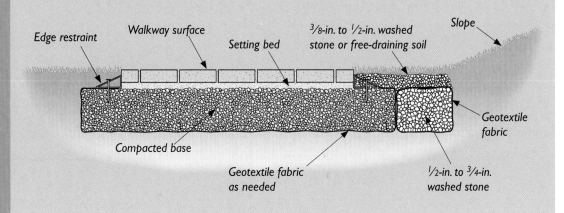

Edge restraint

Walkway surface

Setting bed

$3/8$-in. to $1/2$-in. washed stone or free-draining soil

Slope

Compacted base

Geotextile fabric as needed

$1/2$-in. to $3/4$-in. washed stone

Geotextile fabric

Install geotextile filter fabric before the base if you have moist soil.

prevents small particles of soil from infiltrating and compromising the base material. Overlap any seams by about 24 in., and run the fabric up the sides of the excavation. The excess can be trimmed off after the base is installed.

Installing the base

Like the foundation for a house, a properly installed base is crucial for the long-term integrity of patios and walkways. It provides a stable platform and buffers patios and walkways from the effects of weather.

Three important components that determine the quality of a base are the type of material, amount of compaction, and thickness of the base. A good base material should be free of organic material, drain easily, and compact well. Processed, or crushed, gravel, in which the larger stones are broken up into smaller pieces at the gravel pit, is an excellent base material. Another excellent choice is a product made with recycled materials such as asphalt and concrete, which are sometimes mixed with processed gravel. The specific materials vary from region to region and even yard to yard and are sold under different names. In my region, this product is known as "hard pack." Your local supplier should be able to tell you what it's called in your area.

The best base material will not do its job, however, unless it's properly compacted. Base materials compact more easily and effectively when they contain the "right" amount of moisture. But what's too dry, what's too wet, and what is "right"? Here's a simple test you can use to find the answer. Squeeze a handful of base material into a ball. If it falls apart, it's probably too dry. If it holds its shape, it probably has the right amount of moisture, but if it oozes water, it's probably too wet.

Base materials can be compacted with a hand tamper or with a motorized mechanical compactor. Hand-tamping is tiring and slow going, so it is typically used only in hard-to-reach places, such as corners and against foundations. Plate compactors are easy to use and can cover the larger areas associated with patios and walkways relatively quickly. Regardless of the compacting method, the base material should be compacted in small increments, or "lifts." When hand-tamping, you should compact lifts of 1 in. to

PRO TIP

Geotextile fabrics are much stronger (and more expensive) than so-called "weed blocker" fabrics, which should not be used as an alternate to geotextile fabrics.

PRO TIP

Rake the base material out smoothly before it's compacted to help it compact as evenly as possible.

When using a hand tamper, be sure to hold it perfectly vertically and strike with the entire surface of the metal plate.

Although a mechanical plate compactor is heavy and difficult to move when it's turned off, when it's running it is pulled along by the forward motion created by the vibrating action.

PRO**TIP**

Before compacting the base material, run the plate compactor over the subsoil below the base to compact any material loosened during excavation.

COMPACTING PATIO PAVERS

Start at one edge and compact around the perimeter. Then, working back and forth and overlapping each pass about 4 in. to 6 in., compact the entire surface. Turn 90 degrees and repeat the process. Make two or three passes at 90 degrees and be sure that each paver is compacted at least three times.

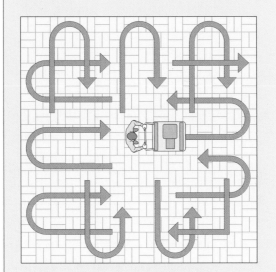

2 in., whereas a mechanical compactor can handle 3-in. to 4-in. lifts.

When using a plate compactor, take your time to compact the base thoroughly. Compact walkways by working along the length of the walk, overlapping each pass by a few inches. For patios, compact thoroughly in one direction and then at 90 degrees, also overlapping each pass (see the drawing at left). Compact each lift until it appears that it cannot be compacted any more.

Manufacturers generally recommend a minimum base thickness of 6 in. for patios and walkways. Because the combined thickness of the setting bed and paving material is usually from 2 in. to 4 in., the typical 12-in.-deep excavation results in a more than adequate 8-in.- to 10-in.-thick base. In regions that don't need to be dug that deep, the excavation should be at least deep enough to accommodate a 6-in. base.

Final layout

After the base has been installed, do the final layout for your patio or walkway, which will guide the installation of the finish material.

Return to or reestablish the reference points, then measure from these points to establish the location of your patio or walkway. If you are using stakes and strings to define the edges of your project, keep in mind that you may have to install some of the stakes, such as those that define the corners, beyond the finished edges so that they aren't disturbed during construction. If you are laying out curves, use the hose or "eyeballing" methods described in "Making an Initial Layout" (on p. 30). You need to be more accurate here than you may have been for the initial layout. Then paint the outline of the patio or walkway.

When the setting bed is installed, it extends beyond, and covers, the painted lines, making it difficult to locate the edge of the patio or walkway. To alleviate this problem, place a series of pin flags at regular intervals along all the lines before installing the setting bed. These flags will project above the setting bed to guide the installation of the finish material.

Painting the lines on the base to outline your walkway can be exciting. It may be the first time it's delineated so vividly, creating the illusion of the finished project.

TRADE SECRET

Laying out circles, or segments of circles, on the ground mainly hinges on determining where you want the center of the circle/segment— the radius point—to be. Sometimes the radius point can be located with precise measurements using tape measures (see p. 59); in other cases, finding it is a matter of trial and error (see p. 96).

You can also lay out a curve by swinging a tape measure from a fixed point and painting the curve as you go.

Creating Right Angles

TO BE MORE ACCURATE WHILE DOING THE FINAL LAYOUT, use the 3-4-5 triangulation method to create right angles. The Pythagorean theorem ($A^2 + B^2 = C^2$) describes the relationship among the three sides of a right triangle (a right triangle has two 45-degree angles and one 90-degree angle). Right triangles with one side 3 ft. long (A) and another 4 ft. long (B) will have a third side (C, the hypotenuse) that's 5 ft. long. Multiples of these distances (6, 8, 10, for example) also create 90-degree angles.

Use the 3-4-5 triangle to create a line, like the edge of a patio, that's perpendicular to your house.

1. Choose a multiple of 3 (for example, 4 ft.), and measure the shortest side of the triangle, 12 ft. (3 x 4 ft.), against the house wall or foundation (see the drawing below).

2. Determine the next side of the triangle by multiplying 4 ft. by the second multiplier, 4, and pull a tape measure from the corner of the house out 16 ft. (4 x 4 ft.).

3. Find the length of the last side of the triangle, the hypotenuse, by multiplying 4 ft. by the third multiplier, 5, and from the 12-ft. mark pull a tape out diagonally 20 ft. (5 x 4 ft.) and cross the first tape at the 16-ft. mark. Install a stake at the intersection of the 16-ft. and 20-ft. marks. The line from this stake to the corner is 90 degrees (a right angle) to the house.

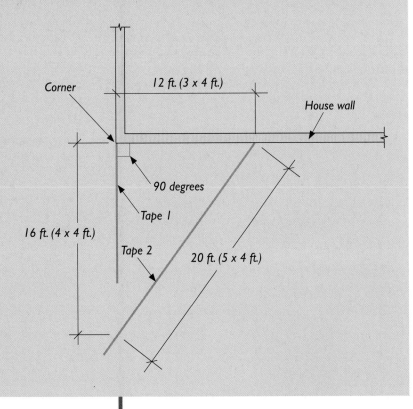

Corner

12 ft. (3 x 4 ft.)

House wall

90 degrees

Tape 1

16 ft. (4 x 4 ft.)

Tape 2

20 ft. (5 x 4 ft.)

Installing the setting bed

The final piece of prep work before laying down the finished surface is to install the setting bed. All dry-laid materials—rough- and cut-stone flagging, concrete and brick pavers—are placed on top of a setting bed. Two types of material are typically used for setting beds—stone dust and sand. Both can be used underneath all types of stone, but concrete and brick paver manufacturers recommend using concrete sand under their pavers. It is coarser than stone dust and other sands, so it drains more quickly and is less likely to spread out over time.

Materials of uniform thickness—such as cut stone flagging and concrete or brick pavers—are installed over a setting bed that's a uniform thickness. (Unlike the base, uniform-thickness setting beds are not compacted as they're installed.) A 1-in.-thick setting bed is generally recommended. To get the correct thickness, lay 1-in. pipes on top of the base. When you installed the base material you created the proper pitch, but you must maintain that pitch as you install the pipes. Use a level to check the pitch before installing the setting bed, and hammer the pipes to adjust their pitch as necessary (see the top photo on the facing page). Additionally, if the patio or walkway is level in one direction, adjust the pipes accordingly. Fill the area with sand up to the top of the pipes, and remove the excess (a process called "screeding").

Irregular stone for patios and walkways varies in thickness, typically from 1 in. to 3 in. In addition, stones are heavy and are either shaped in place (while on the setting bed) or positioned and removed multiple times while being fitted. The setting beds for these stones are inevitably disturbed and do not need to be a uniform thickness. They do, however, need to be at least

Spending money on screeding pipes, something you'll probably never use again, is nonetheless an extremely wise investment. There's really no better way to create a setting bed of the appropriate thickness.

1 in. thicker than the thickest piece of stone that will be used. Before you set the height of the base, determine the thickness of the stones you are using and plan accordingly.

Installing the finish material

After the setting bed has been prepared, the next step is to install the finish material. Although each type of material has its idiosyncrasies, the overall process is similar.

Laying pavers The first task is to decide where to begin laying the pavers, which is different for uniform pavers and irregularly shaped stone flagging. When installing concrete, brick, and cut-stone flaggings, begin in the middle and work toward the edges. For large areas, such as patios, it's important to use a string that bisects the middle to guide your work (see the photo at right). This will keep the joints aligned and running true. It's also important to spend extra time laying the first few rows of pavers to make sure that you begin accurately. Errors here can compound themselves later on.

Because each piece of irregularly shaped stone flagging is custom-fit to the adjacent stone or

It's important that guide strings remain taut, which means that when you install the stakes to tie them, those stakes are driven in solidly and won't be tipped over when stressed by the strings.

stones, the starting point is less crucial. However, if you will be installing stone against a wall or in a corner, it's usually best to start from those straight edges and work out from there. Fitting irregularly shaped stone is time consuming, particularly if you're striving for tight joints, so don't get frustrated if your progress feels glacial. You'll get faster and better with practice, so enjoy the process.

Because irregular stone flagging is not uniform in thickness, when you first lay the stones,

Concrete Paver Patterns

CONCRETE PAVERS are available in a wide variety of shapes and sizes and they can be arranged in an almost endless array of patterns. These drawings illustrate several popular patterns, which can also be used with brick pavers provided they are the same shape.

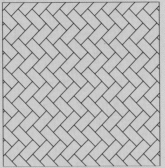

45-degree herringbone

90-degree herringbone

Running bond

Basket weave

Whorling square

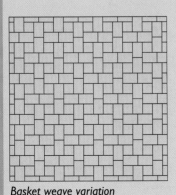

Basket weave variation

Pattern with squares

When working alone, you need to find ways to "grow" an extra hand or two. Tying a string to a rock so you can pull it taut is one way to do that.

some may be above or below the desired surface plane of the patio or walkway. As each stone is installed, use a level, straightedge, or string to check the alignment.

Borders Incorporating a border visually defines the outside edges and adds a decorative element to a patio or walkway. Depending on the desired effect, a border can be made of the same or different material as the patio or walkway. The border of a concrete, brick, or cut-stone paver patio or walkway serves another function: It also works in tandem with the edge restraint to help secure the small cut-paver pieces that inevitably occur at the edges.

Edge restraints Edge restraints are an essential part of installing concrete and brick pavers and cut-stone flagging. Not only do they hold the pavers in place, but they also restrain the setting bed, preventing it from spreading out over time. Although some manufacturers suggest installing the edge restraints before installing the pavers, many pros find it easier and more effective to install them afterwards.

Edge restraints should be installed directly on the base, not on the setting bed. After the pavers

Edge restraints, shown above left and above, come with different profiles and types of spikes. Be sure to follow the manufacturer's recommendation for the number and spacing of the spikes.

are installed, remove the excess sand at the paver's edge with a trowel and scrape it down to the base. Then, securely nail the restraints in place with the spikes provided. The edge restraints are installed so that their tops are below the patio or walkway surface and are hidden from view when the job is finished.

Compacting pavers After flagstones are put down, they are secured in place by their own weight, by stepping on them firmly, or by tapping them with a rubber mallet or, in the case of heavy, thick stones, with an iron bar shielded with a block of wood (see the bottom photo at right).

Concrete and brick pavers, on the other hand, must be compacted with a mechanical plate compactor. As the pavers are compacted, they settle in the setting bed and sand works its way up between the pavers, locking them in place.

Sweep the surface clean of any debris, then spread a thin layer of bedding sand evenly over the pavers. This sand will protect the pavers from being abraded by the compactor as it runs over the surface. Adjust the speed of the compactor so that it runs at a high vibration and at low ampli-

The last thing you want to do is break a piece of flagging that you've already installed, so be sure your aim is true so that you hit the wood block and not the paver.

tude (up-and-down motion) to avoid putting extra stress on the pavers. See the drawing on p. 38 for the pattern to follow as you move around the patio.

Filling the joints Filling the joints is the final task that you must do to complete your patio or walkway. Although joints can be filled with a number of granular materials, the three most

TRADE SECRET

Large patio stones are difficult to handle, so when positioning them it's smart to minimize the number of times you have to lift them. When small adjustments in height need to be made, use a pry bar or hammer claw to pry up the end of the stone needing the adjustment. Add or remove base material under the stone, and set the stone back in place. Check the alignment with a level or straightedge.

tions printed on the bag, but there are a few general points to keep in mind. Be sure to clean the paver surface completely of small bits of leaves, twigs, and dirt. Otherwise, they may be swept into the joints and become a permanent feature. Before pouring out the polymeric sand and spreading it on your patio or walkway, the pavers must be completely dry because the sand will bond to a wet surface. It's all right if the setting bed is damp. After sweeping the sand into the joints but before wetting it, be sure that there are no grains of sand left on the pavers, particularly next to the joints (see the photo at left).

Walls

Walls have been a part of the human environment since we first began to build, and they continue to be an important part of our residential landscapes. They mark boundaries and edges, sculpt the landscape, and add a visually dynamic and beautiful element to our surroundings. The two general kinds of walls—freestanding and retaining—typically are constructed with either dry-laid or mortared techniques. Dry-laid walls, which are the type covered in this book, rely on their own weight, friction, and proper construction techniques to hold together.

Historically, stone has been the material of choice for dry-laid walls. Although rounded, "field" stones can be used, they are difficult to work with. Stones with a more rectangular profile and a grain that splits easily, such as mica schist or sandstone, are a better choice and are used for the projects in this book. Because virtually every stone is a different size and shape, each one has to be custom-fit, which makes building a dry-stone wall relatively time consuming. And it also takes a bit of an artist's eye to create a pleasing arrangement of stones.

common choices are stone dust, concrete sand, and polymeric sand. The type of joint material you choose depends on the type of paver material. For irregular flagstone, stone dust is often used, but sand works well too. The wide joints typically used for cut-stone flagging can also be filled with stone dust or sand, but the tightly spaced joints of concrete and brick pavers must be filled with some type of sand. Sand fills the joints easily and completely, locking the pavers in place. While concrete sand can be used for this application, polymeric sand, which can also be used in wider joints, offers some distinct advantages.

Polymeric sand is a mixture of mason-grade sand and a polymeric additive. When activated with water, the polymeric sand sets up, forming a firm but flexible one-piece barrier. Unlike concrete sand, polymeric sand does not wash away easily, it prevents water from infiltrating the setting bed, and it resists weed growth. Polymeric sand is available in a wide range of colors and can be matched to the pavers.

When installing polymeric sand, it's extremely important to follow the manufacturer's instruc-

The past 10 to 20 years have seen a dramatic rise in the popularity of dry-stacked concrete block walls. Due to their modular design—blocks are uniform in size—these walls go up much faster than stone walls. They are manufactured in myriad styles and colors and can be used to build straight and curved retaining or freestanding walls. Depending on how the blocks are made, the precise installation techniques can vary with each manufacturer and are usually illustrated in literature provided by the supplier or directly from the manufacturer.

Construction sequence

The construction sequence for both dry-laid stone (dry-stone) and concrete block (dry-stacked) walls follows the same basic three-step process and employs techniques similar to those used for building patios and walkways.

Establishing heights and layout After the site is cleared and prepared, the first step is to lay out the stone wall. One important thing to keep in mind is that dry-stone retaining walls are typically constructed with a batter, which means that their faces slope in, usually about 1 in. for every foot of height (see p. 97). Block walls can also be built so that they slope in. When a batter is used, you have to account for it when you lay out the walls.

Excavate and install the base Both dry-stone and dry-stacked walls are built to be flexible and move with small changes of the freeze-and-thaw cycles, so their bases don't need to be below the frost line. However, a stable, well-draining base is a crucial part of constructing a well-built wall, so the excavation must be wide and deep enough to accommodate a proper base.

(see p. 97)

Even if a retaining wall needs to be only about 12 in. high, consider raising it to about 18 in. This height is perfect for sitting on, so your wall can do double duty.

When building a dry-stacked retaining wall, you must install at least some portion of the first course of concrete block below the finish grade. Although recommendations vary with manufacturers and types of block, a rule of thumb is that for walls 2 ft. or lower, bury one half of the first course, and for walls 2 ft. to 4 ft., bury a full course.

You should dig deep enough to remove the topsoil, roots, and any large rocks and so that you can install at least 6 in. of base material. It's best to dig until you reach a granular-type soil, but this is not always practical. If you can't, or if you are building on poor-draining or non-granular soils, a 9-in. to 12-in. gravel base is recommended.

For retaining walls, the first course of stone or concrete block should be installed below the line of the finish grade, so the excavation has to be deep enough to account for this. The excavation should also be wide enough to allow for the installation of crushed stone behind the wall, which allows water to drain away. If you will be building on sloped ground, step the excavation up the slope (see the drawings on p. 47 and p. 51).

After excavating, but before installing the base material, use a mechanical plate compactor to thoroughly compact any soil that may have been disturbed. Then, lay geotextile fabric in the bottom of the trench (and up the side of the embankment for a retaining wall), overlapping the pieces by 12 in.

Next, install the base material (processed or crushed gravel and trap-rock screenings are good choices) over the fabric, compacting in lifts the same way as it's done for patios and walkways.

Build the dry-stone You can start your dry-stone wall anywhere along the prepared base, but it's usually a good idea to begin at an end or, if it will be built against the house, at the foundation. Choose some of the larger stones and arrange them at the proper width along the base, fitting them together like a puzzle. The inside edges of these stones don't have to be tight together and, because the first course or two will be below the grade, you can use stones that have broken or uneven faces.

As you lay each stone, make sure that they are level along their lengths. When building a retaining wall, you can tip the stones backward slightly toward the hill to help create the desired batter. However, this can cause problems if a retaining wall transitions into a freestanding wall or is exposed at one end, such as at a set of stairs. To avoid this problem, keep the stones level front to back and achieve the batter by setting each succeeding course slightly in from the one below it

You can slice holes in geotextile fabric so that it slides over the tops of stakes. Overlap the pieces by at least 12 in. and make sure that they are long enough to do the job. Any excess can be trimmed off later, but trying to add additional fabric is not practical.

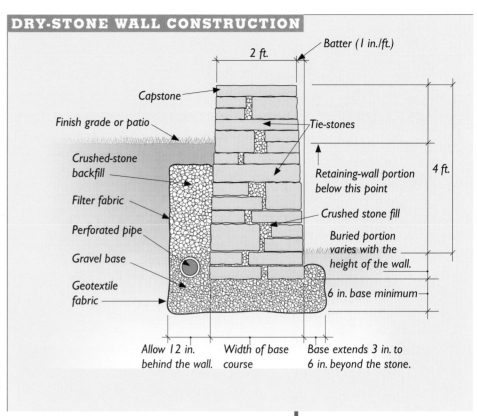

DRY-STONE WALL CONSTRUCTION

Batter (1 in./ft.)

2 ft.

Capstone

Finish grade or patio

Tie-stones

Crushed-stone backfill

Filter fabric

Perforated pipe

Gravel base

Geotextile fabric

Retaining-wall portion below this point

4 ft.

Crushed stone fill

Buried portion varies with the height of the wall.

6 in. base minimum

Allow 12 in. behind the wall.

Width of base course

Base extends 3 in. to 6 in. beyond the stone.

Filling the area between the faces of a double-sided wall is quicker and saves money because you don't need to use relatively expensive wall stone where it won't be seen.

(see the drawing above). Or, if a stone has a sloping face, orient it so that it slopes up and in from the bottom to the top of the stone.

When you finish the base course, fill the spaces between the base stones and the excavation and between each stone with ¾-in. crushed stone or trap rock (see the drawing above). This helps with drainage and to support the upper courses. If the area is particularly wet, install perforated pipe wrapped in filter fabric at the bottom course.

With the base course complete, continue to build the wall. As you proceed, mix up the sizes of the stones. Don't try to make uniform courses

with stones of the same thickness butting against each other, but rather create the level plane by stacking two or three thinner stones next to a thicker one. However, avoid continuous vertical joints; stagger the joints by overlapping the stones every course or two (see the drawing above). Trim or shim each stone as needed to fit, keeping each course running level. From time to time, install a stone that is long enough to span from the front to the back of the wall. These tie-stones help to hold the wall together and are particularly important at the ends of the walls. If you are building a freestanding wall or when your retaining wall transitions into a freestanding wall, you will have to create finished faces on both sides of the wall.

As you near the top of the wall, install the capstones. Start at one end and work along the length of the wall. Because the capstones will probably not all be the same thickness, you'll

Notice the mix of thick and thin stones and how several thin stones are used next to thicker ones. The several small stones are also used against the round accent rock.

To save time and get a more accurate fit, depending on the type of stone you're using, you may be able to trim capstones in place. Just be sure to go slowly so that you don't overtrim them.

In addition to including tie-stones from front to back in your wall, run some long stones in the direction of the wall as well. These stones introduce a nice horizontal line to the wall and visually and physically tie the shorter stones together.

Keep a selection of small "shim" stones roughly sorted by size close at hand in plastic 5-gallon buckets.

have to vary the height of the wall beneath them. Choose the first two or three capstones and measure their thicknesses. Measure down from the top-of-the-wall mark on the foundation, or from the guide string, the thickness of the first capstone and build the wall up to that point. To overlap the joints, extend the end of the top wall stone a little beyond the first capstone. Lay the capstone in place and shim it as necessary. Continue in this manner, measuring the stone, building up the wall to the proper height, and placing the capstone, until the wall is finished. You can take small pieces

of stones and fill in the gaps to suit your eye (see the bottom right photo above).

Build the concrete-block wall Unlike a dry-stone wall, it's important to begin your concrete-block wall at a fixed point, such as a foundation wall. If your wall has 90-degree corners, it's best to start there. The first course of block is the most crucial, so take your time with it.

Position the first block and level it front to back and side to side. Then lay the rest of the blocks in the first course, and use a string or long straightedge to make sure that their faces are

Working with Stone

THERE ARE THREE TECHNIQUES you need to know when working with irregular flagging or wall stone: splitting, breaking, and truing.

You can split stones to make them fit into narrower spaces and create two stones out of one very thick stone. Stones with distinct layers or seams split best. Find a seam that's closest to the thickness you're trying to create, and using a wide-bladed stonemason's chisel, score along the length of the seam with relatively light blows with a 2-lb. or 3-lb. sledgehammer. Continue this process, using stronger hits and moving the chisel after each blow. As the crack begins to open, ease off, but continue hammering until the stone splits.

Hitting it just with a sledgehammer can break a stone, but the results are usually unpredictable. To break a piece of stone to a particular size or shape requires a little more finesse. Using either a wide-bladed chisel or the tapered end of a stonemason's hammer, score a line. As with splitting, continue working along the line with firm blows until the stone breaks. Be careful not to hit the stone too hard or the stone might break where you don't want it to. Experience will tell you what's too hard.

Rough stones often have bumps or protrusions that have to be removed to create a flat surface. To true a stone, position a chisel at the base of the area you want to remove, tilting the chisel at about a 45-degree angle. Repeatedly strike the chisel with a hammer until the surface is smooth. Depending on the type of stone, the protrusion may pop off in one piece or have to be broken off in smaller chunks.

When splitting a stone, take your time. Trying to rush the job often means breaking, not splitting, the stone.

As you get experienced breaking stones, you may find you get in a pleasant rhythm, much like that of a blacksmith working wrought iron.

When truing a stone, it's easy to scrape a knuckle or a finger, so it's a good idea to wear gloves.

Blocks with pins can be a little more difficult to install than those with tongues and grooves. If you find it hard to install heavy blocks with pins, enlist the aid of a helper.

To avoid having excess adhesive ooze out of the tube after you've stopped squeezing, get a caulking gun that has a quick-release trigger, which, with the click of a finger, eases off on the plunger.

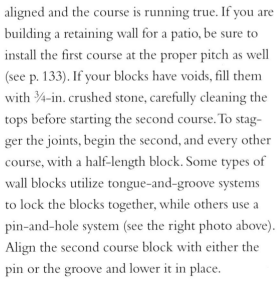

PRO**TIP**

To make installing
the first course easier,
you can lightly loosen the
first ½ in. of base material or spread ½ in. of sand
on the base.

aligned and the course is running true. If you are building a retaining wall for a patio, be sure to install the first course at the proper pitch as well (see p. 133). If your blocks have voids, fill them with ¾-in. crushed stone, carefully cleaning the tops before starting the second course. To stagger the joints, begin the second, and every other course, with a half-length block. Some types of wall blocks utilize tongue-and-groove systems to lock the blocks together, while others use a pin-and-hole system (see the right photo above). Align the second course block with either the pin or the groove and lower it in place.

After you have built two or three courses, fill the area behind blocks with ¾-in. crushed stone (see the drawing on p. 51). If the area is particularly wet, install perforated pipe wrapped in filter fabric at the bottom course. Continue until you

have laid the last course of block. You can install the rest of the crushed stone now or wait until after you install the cap. Wrap the fabric over the top of the stone. Once the wall is finished, backfill over the fabric with soil.

The final step is to install the cap. To avoid having a lot of the cap joints lining up with block joints, lay out the cap before you glue it and get the alignment correct, cutting the first piece to a length that works best. The cap pieces are held in place with a special construction-grade adhesive formulated for use with concrete. Apply two or three ½-in.-wide beads to the top of the block course and press the caps in place. (see the photo above right). So that the adhesive doesn't skin over, only do three or four blocks at a time. Allow the adhesive to completely cure, about 24 hours or so, and your wall is finished.

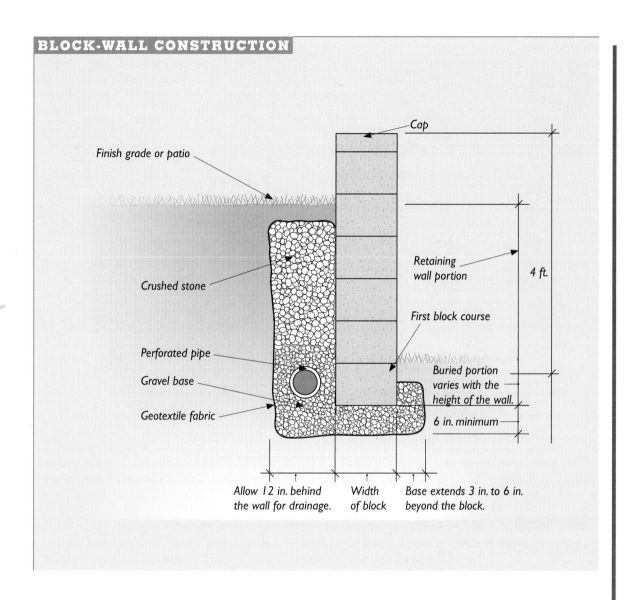

Cap

Finish grade or patio

Crushed stone

Retaining
wall portion

4 ft.

First block course

Perforated pipe

Gravel base

Geotextile fabric

Buried portion
varies with the
height of the wall.

6 in. minimum

Allow 12 in. behind
the wall for drainage.

Width
of block

Base extends 3 in. to 6 in.
beyond the block.

Steps

It's the rare house that's built with the first floor one step above the ground or on land that is perfectly flat. As a result, steps are often an indispensable part of the residential landscape and often constructed in conjunction with patios and walkways. In addition to their functional qualities, they can add a sense of movement and flair to their surroundings.

Steps can be categorized by their method of construction—riser only, one-piece, infill tread, mortared, and dry laid. The general concepts that govern stair design and construction are basically the same for all types of steps; however, we will focus on two types of dry-laid steps—dry-stone and dry-stacked concrete block.

Step terminology

To design and build steps, there are four essential concepts that you need to understand—rise, run, riser, and tread. Rise and run are units of measure, whereas riser and tread are physical components of a set of steps.

Rise is a vertical measurement. The *total rise* is the distance from the bottom to the top of the

steps, and the *unit of rise* is the height of an individual step, from the bottom of the step to the top of the tread. A *riser* is the face of the step that spans the unit of rise, less the thickness of the tread.

Run is a measure of horizontal distance. The *total run* is the overall length of the entire set of steps and the *unit of run* is the length, or depth, of an individual step. A *tread* is the horizontal stepping surface.

There's a related concept, *pitch*, which is expressed as a ratio of the unit of rise to the unit of run and is used to define the steepness of a set of steps. The relationship between the rise and run is extremely important and, for practical and safety reasons, it falls within a relatively narrow range. To be comfortable, the rise for outdoor steps, which can be lower than for interior stairs, should be from 5 in. to 7 in. And, as a general rule, as the unit of rise increases, the unit of run decreases, and vice versa.

There's a formula that is used for landscape stairs to calculate this relationship and the respective distances—two times the rise plus the run equals 26 in. (2Ri + Ru = 26 in.). For example, a rise of 7 in. results in a run of 12 in. [26 − (2 × 7) = 12], while a 6-in. rise creates a 14-in. run [26 − (2 × 6) = 14].

Construction sequence

The construction sequence for both dry-stone and dry-stacked follow the same basic three-step process, and the techniques for the steps covered here are similar to those used for patios, walkways, and walls.

Determine the total rise and do the layout The first task when planning a set of steps is to determine the total rise, from which you calculate the number and dimensions of the risers and treads. Using a level, line level, or builder's level, find the distance the stairs must span, from the bottom to the top. Divide that figure by a number that represents a comfortable riser height, for example, 6. If it works out to be a whole number, 3 for instance, then that's the number of risers and 6 in. is the height of each riser. If it's a fraction, 6½ in., for example, divide the nearest whole number, 3, into the total rise to get the size of the riser.

Then, using the formula given on the facing page, calculate the length of the tread. If you will be building the steps into a hillside, you may have to adjust the rise and run to work with the slope. Note that in any given flight of steps, there is always one fewer tread than the number of risers.

After you've calculated their length and settled on the width of the steps, lay them out on the ground. Use strings and stakes to mark their location, offsetting them so that they are outside the area to be excavated. As with patios and walkways, the excavated area and base should extend about 6 in. outside the area of the steps.

Excavate and install the base Both dry-stone and dry-stacked concrete block steps are built to be flexible and move with small changes of the freeze-and-thaw cycles, so their bases don't

need to be below the frost line. See the section on constructing base walls on p. 45 for more information on how to construct bases for steps.

If you build an above-grade set of steps, one that rises above the surrounding ground, only the first step has a base that's built into the ground. The rest of the base is created by filling underneath the steps. However, whether you are filling in the area underneath the steps or building on a hillside, install and compact the base as you build each step (see the drawing below).

When the base for the first step is installed, you are ready to build the steps. The process is slightly different for dry-stone and dry-stacked concrete block steps.

Build dry-stone steps Before you start building the first riser, choose the stones that you

PRO**TIP**

If your steps will have an overhang, or nosing, the amount of the overhang is added to the size of the run to get the overall depth of the tread.

RISE AND RUN

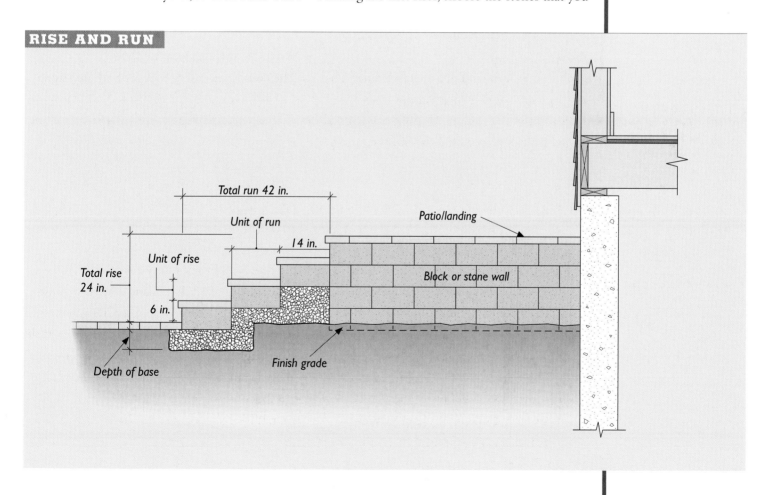

Total run 42 in.

Unit of run

14 in.

Patio/landing

Unit of rise

Total rise 24 in.

6 in.

Block or stone wall

Finish grade

Depth of base

Typically, the same
concrete blocks and
capstones that are used
for wall construction
are used to build steps.
Choose a style of block
that offers the size that
works best for your rise/
run situation. Or, if possible, adjust the height of
the total rise.

want to use for treads. Because each succeeding riser is supported on the tread below, the treads should be at least 2 in. longer than the unit of run, plus any overhang.

Measure the thickness of the stone you've chosen for the first tread. Build the first riser, leveling it front to back and side to side, so that the height of the riser plus the tread equals the unit of rise. Fill the area behind the riser stones with small pieces of stone and base material. This helps to fully support the tread. Install the tread, trimming and squaring the front and sides as necessary.

Next, compact a level section of base behind the first tread and build the second riser so that its face is supported on the first tread. Again,

measure the thickness of the second tread and build the riser to the right height to accommodate it. Install the second tread as before. Continue building in this way until you complete the final tread.

Build dry-stacked steps Unlike dry-stone steps, all the riser blocks for dry-stacked steps are installed before the treads. This reduces the possibility of damaging the treads during construction and results in a tighter joint by allowing the treads to be fit directly against the face of the risers.

Arrange the blocks for the first riser—leveling them side to side and front to back—on the compacted base. Make sure that the tops of the

Instead of being staggered, the joints in the treads of these dry-stacked steps are aligned with each other, which lends an air of formality to this straight-run stair.

A good rule of thumb is to take a little extra time to get the first course of a wall or set of steps right. That's particularly true when installing dry-stone risers. Here, not only should the stones be level but also their tops aligned with each other.

blocks are at the proper height above the finish grade or walkway to create the correct unit of rise. Don't forget to account for the tread.

Fill the area behind the first riser with base material and compact it thoroughly, bringing it to proper height. Using a half-wide block to offset the joints, set the top of the second at the unit of rise above the first riser. This time you don't have to account for the tread thickness because this and all succeeding risers are automatically increased when the tread is installed. Continue installing risers in this manner until all of them are installed.

Before moving on to the next step, double-check to make sure all the risers are still level and at the correct height. If your riser blocks have voids in them, fill the voids with base material and sweep all the tops completely clean.

To finish the steps, install the treads, which are typically composed of several pieces. The treads are held in place with a construction-grade adhesive formulated for use with concrete. To avoid disturbing the treads after they've been set, install them from the top down. You can work from a piece of plywood placed on the risers below to avoid disturbing them.

Before gluing the treads down, arrange the first tread on the riser blocks and check for fit and any overhang. Take them off and apply two or three ½-in.-wide beads of adhesive to the top of the riser blocks and press the treads firmly in place. Move down to the next tread. Offsetting the joints may require that you cut a tread piece. Glue as before and continue until all the treads are done. Allow the adhesive to completely cure, about 24 hours or so, before walking on the steps.

FORMAL FRONT WALKWAY

When guests park in your driveway, you want to make a good impression as they make their way to your front door. If you have a long walk, this can be tricky. A long, straight walk can be too dull, while a walk with lots of curves can seem odd and random. The solution is to match your walkway to your house shape and style.

The sinuous walkway in this chapter curves in to reflect the angle of the garage and out again to meet the semicircular landing that fronts the entry stairs. To complement the formal style of the house, the same cut bluestone that graces the entry steps is used for the walkway. Cut bluestone is relatively smooth and uniform, providing an even walking surface that's perfect for a front walkway. If you'd like to add a bit of flair and formality to your house, a bluestone walkway might be a perfect fit. ▶ ▶ ▶

Prepare the Site

Sometimes determining the best time to build a walkway can be a challenge, particularly if you're remodeling the house at the same time or if your house is still under construction. To avoid the possibility of disturbing the prepared site, or walking or placing heavy objects on an unfinished walkway, make sure that certain tasks—such as trim, siding work, painting, and extensive plantings—are completed before beginning the walkway. And before doing the initial layout, the foundation should be backfilled and the finished grade in the area surrounding the walkway should be set. If your walkway will be constructed in an existing lawn, you won't have these issues.

Initial walkway layout

This walkway is 4 ft. wide along its length. To create a more inviting entrance, though, at the beginning and where it intersects the side of the landing, the walkway flares out to 6 ft.

1. After the finished grade is set, the first layout task is to locate the beginning of the walkway. Measure out the distance from the corner of the garage to the walkway as indicated on the plan—6 ft. for this walk—and install stake A.

2. Measure the width of the entrance of the walkway, and install another stake, B. (See **A** and the drawing below.)

WALKWAY LAYOUT

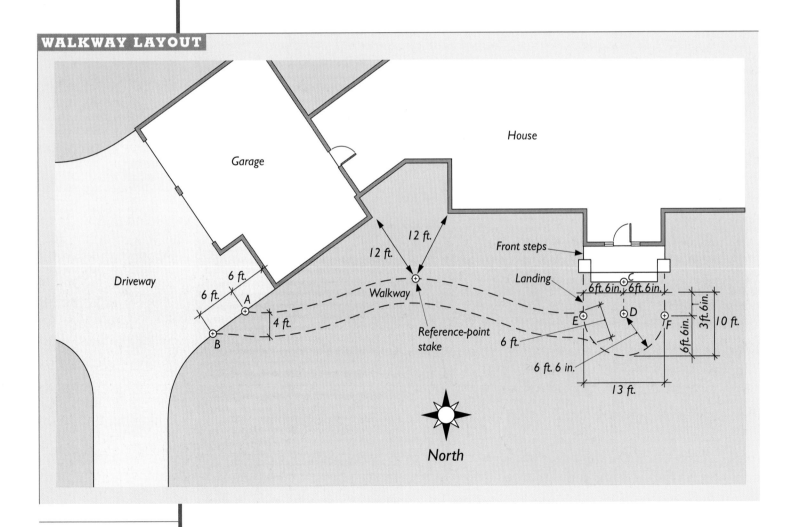

Initial landing layout

The next layout task is to mark out the landing portion of the walkway. This landing is 10 ft. deep and consists of a semicircle, plus a short straight section. The radius of the semicircle is equal to one half of the width of the stairs, 6 ft. 6 in. in this example. To make the overall depth of the landing equal 10 ft., the straight section must be 3 ft. 6 in. long (3 ft. 6 in. + 6 ft. 6 in. = 10 ft.). (See the drawing on the facing page.)

1. Locate the center of the first step, and install stake C or make a mark on the step. This also indicates the center of the landing. Then measure out from the step the length of the straight section, 3 ft. 6 in., and install stake D. This will be the center of the arc. Because this distance is relatively short, you can use a framing square to make sure this measurement is perpendicular to the steps, as shown in **C**. (Longer distances may require the use of the 3-4-5 triangle; see p. 40.) Following the same procedure, install stakes E and F 3 ft. 6 in. out from the ends of the step **D**.

3. Much of this walkway is free-form, or laid out by eye, but it's important to have at least one reference point that can be used to relocate the walkway after the base has been excavated. When this walkway was designed, the curve nearest the house was positioned relative to two corners—one at the garage and another at the house. To mark this reference point, we measured out 12 ft. from each corner and installed a stake where the measuring tapes intersect, as shown in **B**.

PRO TIP

When you're working alone, it can be difficult to hold a tape measure and swing an arc at the same time. Instead, use a string of the correct length tied to the center stake.

2. Pull a tape measure out to the correct radius, 6 ft. 6 in. in this example, and scratch or paint the arc in the dirt **E**. Use paint to mark the arc on grass.

Connect walkway with landing

1. Use a garden hose to lay out the entire length of the path, making sure that the hose touches the reference stake and flares out at the beginning and landing **F**. When you are satisfied with the layout, mark it by scratching a line in the dirt or painting a series of dots along the length of the hose **G**. Remove the hose and,

following the scratched line or connecting the dots, paint a line along this side of the walkway.

2. From the line you just painted, measure out the width of the walkway at points every 2 ft. to 4 ft. along the walkway, account for the flare, and then mark these points.

3. Connect the dots you just made to complete the outline of the walkway, as shown in **H**.

Excavate the site

Although you can dig out a base by hand, it's usually best to excavate with a machine for long walkways like this one. You can hire an excavating contractor to do the work, or rent a piece of equipment—a Bobcat® or skid steer—and do it yourself.

1. To provide proper support, the base for a bluestone walkway should be about 1 ft. wider than the width of the finished walk. So measure out about 6 in. from each side of the walkway lines and paint two additional lines.

2. Excavate the walkway area all the way to the widest lines, as shown in **I**. The depth of excavation varies with soil type and climate (for more on excavating, see p. 34).

3. Compact the subsoil with a mechanical plate compactor **J**.

(for more on excavating, see p. 34).

PRO TIP

With new construction, it's particularly important to compact the subsoil because portions of the ground could have been recently backfilled and may not have been compacted enough.

TRADE SECRET

Water and time are two of the best soil-compacting agents. With new construction, you don't have the time to wait for the subsoil to compact naturally, but you can still make use of water. After compacting the excavated area once, soak it with water, then compact it a second time.

PRO TIP

It's good to have a little extra base material close at hand to quickly fill small low spots that you discover when laying out the pipes.

2. Check the pipes to make sure they are sloping correctly (1.5 percent or 3/16 in. per ft. here) by laying the level along the length of each pipe and adjusting the pipes as necessary. Then make sure the pipes are level with each other at the ends **B**.

3. To temporarily hold the pipes in position, shovel small piles of bedding material onto the ends of the pipes **C**. Then fill the area between and on either side of the pipes with enough bedding material to cover them **D**.

4. Screed the setting bed to create a smooth surface. Using a side-to-side motion, pull the screed toward you, as shown in **E**. After screeding a small section, double-check the height of the setting bed in relation to the step to make

TRADE SECRET

When a project includes a combination of wide and narrow areas, such as a landing and a walkway, it's handy to have screeds of different lengths, perhaps 4 ft., 6 ft., or 8 ft. The longer ones are efficient when used by two people to screed large areas but can be unwieldy for narrow walkways.

PROTIP

Use a trowel to smooth stone dust up against steps. Place an edge against the riser, and pull the excess toward you and off the setting bed.

sure the height is correct . In this project, the distance from the step to the setting bed is 8 in. Continue screeding until you reach the end of the pipes.

5. Remove the pipe nearest the walkway by gently sliding it out of the setting bed. Place that pipe parallel to the remaining pipe, at the edge of the landing. Repeat steps 1 through 4 above until this side of the landing is done too . When you are done, remove the pipes.

6. After the pipes are removed, fill in the voids with bedding material and trowel them smooth . If you can't reach a void without disturbing the setting bed, then don't fill it now. Any remaining voids will be filled in as you install the bluestone.

7. To finish the landing setting bed, place two pipes parallel to each other, perpendicular to the direction of the landing pipes. They should extend into the walkway, staying inside of the painted edges. Place a 4-ft. level on top of the pipes to make sure you have the correct pitch across the width of the walkway, 1.5 percent in this example **I**.

8. You can move on to laying the landing pavers now (see "Lay the Bluestone" below) or install the walkway setting bed.

The walkway

When the landing is complete, install the walkway setting bed. Remember to install only as much as you can cover in one working session.

1. Following the procedure you used in steps 1–7 beginning on p. 63, position the pipes, place and screed the stone dust, remove the pipes, and fill and trowel the voids. Two people may be needed to screed large areas **J**.

2. Once you've finished installing one section of the setting bed, install the pavers to cover it (see "Lay the Bluestone" below). Then move on to install the next section of the setting bed.

Lay the Bluestone

This walkway and landing use a completely random pattern with five different-sized stones—1 ft. by 1 ft., 1 ft. by 2 ft., 18 in. by 18 in., 2 ft. by 2 ft., and 2 ft. by 3 ft.—with ½-in. spacing. A full-random pattern works particularly well with a curved walkway and circular landing like the ones shown here. Adjust the following

PRO**TIP**

To avoid having to set stones from an awkward position, make sure the first stone you set is large enough to stand on while you work.

PRO**TIP**

When installing pavers on wide areas, such as a landing, it's best to start in the middle and work toward the edges. Joints will be less likely to shift out of alignment.

step-by-step procedure as necessary to work with your chosen pattern.

1. Without stepping in the setting bed, position the first flagstone near the middle of the steps and carefully lower it into position, keeping it tight to the riser, as shown in **A**. Settle the stone in place by firmly stepping, but not jumping, on it or by tapping it with a rubber mallet **B**.

2. Lay additional stones to begin the pattern, and set them in place. Use wood spacers the same thickness as your joints to make it easy to keep the correct size joint **C**. When you get close enough to reach any voids in the setting bed left by the pipes that you couldn't reach earlier, fill them with stone dust and trowel them smooth **D**.

3. Although it's not always possible, it's a good idea to avoid using small pieces at the edges. As you approach the ends of the steps, measure

TRADE SECRET

It's difficult to know precisely where the edges of the walk are, so choose stones that are clearly wider than necessary at the edges. The excess will be cut off, and many of the pieces can be used later.

PRO TIP

As you lay down the bluestone, you can leave out some of the smaller pieces at the edges and fill them in later with pieces you cut off the larger stones.

the distance from the end to the previously installed flagstone pavers , then find a combination of pavers to fill that space, using a large paver at the end **F**. With some planning and a rare bit of luck, large, full pieces fit at both ends of these steps.

4. As you're installing the pavers, use a 4-ft. level or other straightedge to check their alignment from time to time **G**. If you encounter a low stone, use a small pry bar to gently lift or remove it altogether and smooth additional stone dust under it with a trowel.

5. Continue laying stones until all of the prepared setting bed has been covered. Stones can extend beyond the layout lines—you'll cut them to the right size later.

Adjusting Spacing

WHEN CUT-STONE PAVERS are manufactured, they are typically sized to allow for a ½-in. joint. For example, while the "nominal" size of a piece may be 12 in. by 12 in., the actual size is about 11¾ in. by 11¾ in. And, although cut stone is theoretically manufactured to specific dimensions, in practice, the actual size can range within certain tolerances set by the manufacturer—typically plus or minus ⅛ in. In addition, sides may be of unequal length, and individual stones may not be perfectly square or rectangular. Therefore, as you lay the pavers, you have to account for these variations by making small adjustments.

To minimize discrepancies, measure the side of a previously laid piece and, for the next one, choose a piece that's close in length. Don't try to match it exactly—it would be time consuming and probably not even possible. The trick is to "split the difference" in length variations. For example, for stones that differ by ⅛ in., move the newly laid stone so that the side of the longer stone projects beyond the side of the shorter by 1⁄16 in. on both ends. Then check the spacing/joints of adjacent pavers and adjust them as necessary.

Wooden spacers can make measuring the joint width easier. However, due to variations in the size of cut flagging, the spaces may sometimes be wider or narrower than the spacer.

Cut the Bluestone

Once all the stones are in place, you need to cut the stones to create the finished edge. When cutting free-form curves and edges that don't butt against a wall, it's faster and more accurate to cut large flagging, such as these bluestone pavers, in place. You can use an electric circular saw equipped with a diamond blade, but we used a gas-powered cut-off saw with a diamond blade. It's faster and can cut tighter curves than a circular saw.

The landing

1. Relocate the center of the landing arc following the process in step 1 on p. 59. Use a string and marking crayon or pencil to outline the edge of the landing **A**.

2. Lightly score the entire line to reduce the possibility of chipping the stone, as shown in **B**. Line up the blade with the score line, then cut the stone all the way through. If you're using a circular saw, you will need to make multiple passes.

3. After all the pavers are cut, fill in any gaps with appropriately sized pieces. Position the pieces, then mark and cut them. If the distance is short, you might be able to freehand the mark **C**; otherwise, use the string and crayon.

Before moving on to the walkway, install the plastic edge restraint at the landing (see p. 72).

WHAT CAN GO WRONG

Circular saws will bind up when cutting a curve. To avoid this problem, you need to make multiple shallow cuts, with each succeeding cut deeper than the previous one. The depth of each cut is determined by the tightness of the curve, with tighter curves requiring shallower cuts.

D

E

F

The walkway

Free-form curves can be difficult to lay out and, because much of it is done by eye, the finished curve probably won't match the rough curve of the base exactly. As long as it looks good to you, that's fine.

1. Starting at the landing, use a piece of the edge restraint to guide your marking crayon as you draw the inside curving edge of the walkway. (Remember that the walkway widens to 6 ft. at this point as well as at the driveway.) Because the edge restraint is flexible, you might need some help shaping and holding it in place **D**. Continue laying out the edge of the walkway in this manner until you reach the end. Then step back and take a look at the shape and adjust it if you don't like it.

2. When you are satisfied with the layout, cut the pavers as explained in steps 2 and 3 on p. 70. Then fill in any spaces with small scrap pieces, marking and cutting them as in step 3 on p. 70.

3. After one side of the walkway has been cut, measure the width of the walkway—6 ft. at the landing and driveway and 4 ft. the rest of the way—and make crayon marks at regular intervals **E**. Align the edge restraint with the marks and draw a line. Cut the pavers **F**, and install any small scrap pieces.

PRO TIP

As you install the spikes, angle them in toward the edge restraints so that as they are hammered home, they pull the restraint in against the pavers.

Install the Edge Restraints

Edge restraints are an essential part of installing bluestone flagging. They hold the smaller pieces in place and prevent the setting bed from spreading out over time. (For more information on edge restraints, see p. 42.)

1. Edge restraints should be installed directly on the base, not on the setting bed. Using a trowel or your hand, remove the setting bed at the edge of the pavers **A**.

2. Position a section of edge restraint and pull it up tight against the pavers. Nail the edge restraint in place with the provided spikes spaced about 1 ft. apart **B**.

3. Attach the second section of edge restraint to the first with the provided clip and nail it in place, as shown in **C**. Continue until all the edge restraint is installed.

Fill the Joints

The joints in this walkway are filled with poly-meric sand. While it's possible to use stone dust to fill the joints, polymeric sand won't get washed out from between the joints as easily and it suppresses weed growth more effectively.

1. After the last section of stone is installed, inspect all the joints to make sure they are free of excess stone dust and extraneous material. If necessary, use a stiff broom to remove excess stone dust and expose most of the full 1-in. thickness of the pavers. Then wet the entire walkway with a hose **A**. This will compact the stone dust and provide a firm base for the poly-meric sand.

2. After the stones have dried completely (it's okay if the stone dust is damp), it's time to fill the joints. Following the manufacturer's direc-

tions, spread some polymeric sand over the stones and sweep it into the joints until they are filled to the top. Clean the surface of all of the polymeric sand, or it may stick to the surface after it's wet and be difficult to remove.

3. Beginning near the steps and the inside edge of the walkway and working in the direction of the pitch, gently spray the entire surface. This will wash away any remaining unseen particles and dust. Be careful not to wash the polymeric sand from between the joints. Manufacturers recommend wetting the sand again after 10 to 15 minutes. Depending on conditions, it may take about 24 hours for it to harden completely. However, these specifics may vary from product to product, so follow the instructions carefully. After the sand has cured, you can backfill and plant the area around the walkway.

WHATCAN GOWRONG

When installing polymeric sand, make sure you sweep the sur-face of the pavers com-pletely free of sand. If you don't, the residual sand will harden on top of the pavers when the pavers are sprayed with water and you'll have a difficult time removing it.

PROTIP

Do not spray the water directly into the joints. This could wash out the polymeric sand from the joints.

BACKYARD MAKEOVER

There comes a time in every family's life when the kids leave home and the parents want to reclaim the house and even the backyard. When playground equipment is no longer needed or out-of-style decks become passé, you can re-create your backyard into a grown-up space you'll want to use all the time.

In this backyard, the small deck and aboveground pool had outlived their usefulness. The solution was to replace the deck with a new screened porch and the pool with a small patio. The new patio—flanked by flower beds that are anchored by large boulders—is located in a sheltered corner of the yard with a short walkway connecting it to the screened porch.

Minimal site preparation work was required for this project. After the deck was demolished and the porch constructed, the pool was removed. The rest of the site prep work consisted of removing the few plantings in, and adjacent to, the location of the new patio and walkway. ▶ ▶ ▶

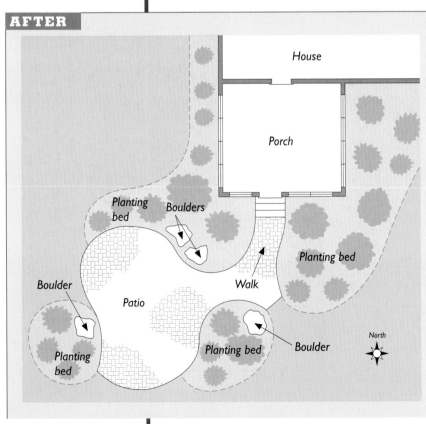

BEFORE

Plantings

House

Deck

Lawn

North

Aboveground pool

AFTER

House

Porch

Planting bed

Boulders

Boulder

Planting bed

Walk

Planting bed

Patio

Boulder

Planting bed

North

Initial Layout and Site Preparation

When a patio is constructed next to a house, rectilinear shapes and straight lines may feel right at home. However, when a patio is surrounded by lawn or gardens, the same forms can look rigid and out of place. In these situations, curves seem more appropriate. This patio is based on a circular shape, but it has a free-form feel. In fact, much of this patio was laid out by eye. However, even a loose form must have a few fixed reference points.

The patio's general overall dimensions are 16 ft. wide and 20 ft. long. The walkway, which is 3 ft. 6 in. wide, curves gently from the steps and intersects the patio at the edge closest to the porch.

To begin, choose a spot that will act as a reference point for the layout, which for this project was the southwest corner of the porch. The edge of the porch is in line with the intersection of the patio and walkway.

1. In line with your reference point, mark the location of one side of the walkway and install stake A. Here we measured 14 ft. from the corner of the porch, our reference point (see the drawing on the facing page). From stake A, measure the width of the walkway and install stake B. The base for concrete paver walkways and patios should be about 12 in. wider than the finished surface, so add that amount to the width of the walkway when you measure. For this project, we measured 4 ft. 6 in. from stakes A and B.

2. Using the end of the walkway as a reference point and to account for the extra width of the base, measure 17 ft. across the width of the

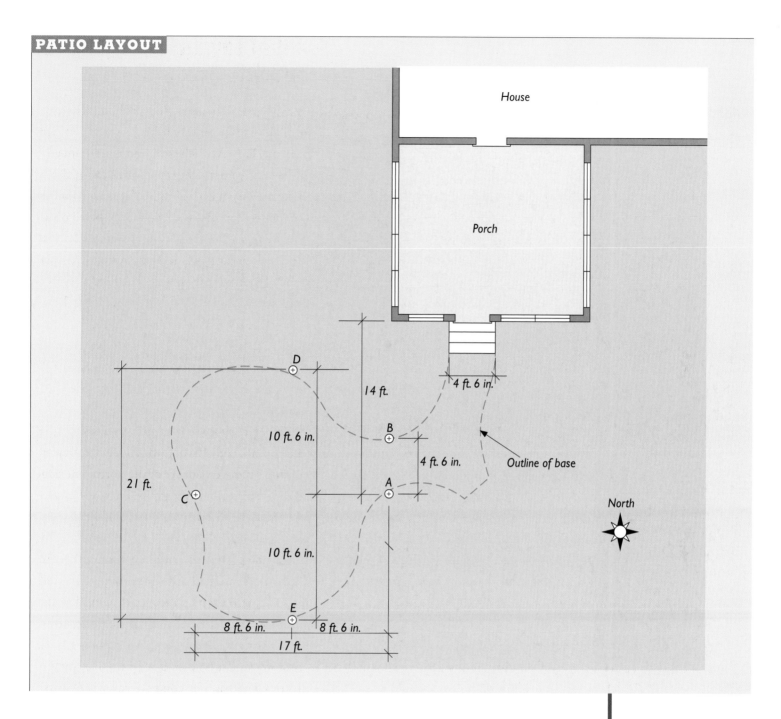

patio from stake A and install stake C. This line is parallel to the front of the porch.

3. The length of the patio is centered on the line between stakes A and C. Find the midpoint between A and C. From there, measure out 10 ft. 6 in. to each side and install two stakes, D and E (see the drawing above).

Although you can remove the plantings and dig out a base by hand, you might find it a good investment to rent a piece of excavating equipment or hire an excavating contractor to do the work. This was particularly true for this project because the washed stone base underneath the pool had to be removed from the site.

1. Remove any plantings that are in the way or that might be damaged during excavation or construction.

2. Excavate the patio and walkway. You can use marking paint to outline the area. The depth of excavation varies with soil type and climate (see p. 34). (No paint was used here because the entire pool area had to be excavated.) In conjunction with removing the material below the pool, the walkway was excavated, and then the heights were established.

3. After the area is excavated, rake any disturbed areas of the subsoil and compact the entire area with a plate compactor **A**.

Establish the Heights

When a patio is constructed in the middle of a lawn, the height of the existing grade largely determines the top of the patio, which should be approximately flush with the surrounding ground. By chance, this lawn slopes toward the south, resulting in a pitch of about ¼ in. per ft. that will help to drain water off of the patio. If your lawn is level, you can raise one end slightly above grade and set the other end at, or slightly below, grade to help shed water. Water will puddle up on a level patio. The top of the walkway is level with the patio at their intersection and slopes uphill toward the steps, where the walkway height is determined by the location of the first riser.

In conjunction with the finish heights of the patio and walkway, the height of the base must be established. Concrete pavers are installed over a compacted base and a sand setting bed. The concrete pavers used for this project are 2⅜ in. thick and are installed on a 1-in. sand setting bed installed on top of the base. When compacted, pavers settle about ⅜ in.

1. Install a reference stake at the stairs. Measure down from the first tread the distance of the riser and mark the stake. Next, measure down the distance to the top of the base. To get the measurement, add the thicknesses of the setting bed and the pavers, then subtract the amount they will settle. For this project, the measurement is: 1 in. + 2⅜ in. – ⅜ in. = 3 in. Mark the stake.

2. If they were removed during the excavation, reset stakes A–E. Using either a line level or a builder's sight level, mark the top of the lawn/patio on the stakes as shown in **A**.

3. Measure down 3 in.—the distance with the pavers compacted—on the stakes to set the top of the base.

Install the Base and the Boulders

After the heights are established, install the base material. A crushed recycled material is used for this project. You can move the base material into place by hand, but it's faster with a Bobcat or skid steer.

1. Install the base material incrementally, in small lifts of about 3 in. to 4 in. each. Spread

A

A

B

C

an even layer of base material over the entire
excavated area, and compact it thoroughly with
a plate compactor **A** and **B**. Continue in this
manner until the base nears the correct height.

2. Once the base is near the correct height,
draw a string from the top-of-patio marks
between the various stakes. Measure down
from the string at different points to check the
height of the base, which should be 3 in. below
the string **C**. Fill any low spots with additional
base material and compact it. Where the com-

pactor cannot reach effectively, such as next to
steps, compact it by hand.

3. When the base is finished, it's a good time
to place the boulders in the planting beds.
Although it's much easier to do with a machine,
as shown in **D**, large rocks can be moved with
the help of hand trucks, planks, and rollers.

4. Wet the entire base **E**. This will help to
compact the base further.

D

E

Do the Final Layout

Although this patio is primarily laid out by eye, you can use your reference stakes as a guide if you need reassurance.

1. Mark one edge of the walkway by painting a series of dots that outline the desired curve. When you're satisfied with the shape, connect the dots with a solid, painted line **A**. Stop painting where the walkway intersects the patio.

2. To establish the proper width of the walkway, measure 3 ft. 6 in. from the inside line to the outside line every 2 ft. to 3 ft., and paint a series of dots **B**. Connect these dots with a painted line.

3. With the walkway marked, outline the patio using the same painting technique in steps 1 and 2. Because all the painted lines will be covered and hidden from view when the setting bed is put down, install pin flags at regular intervals

A

B

along the lines . These flags mark the edge
of the patio (not the edge of the setting bed)
for future reference. At this time you could also
outline any planting beds that will be installed.

4. To do a final check of the base surface,
lay a screeding pipe at various places to see if
there are any low or high spots and fill them
as needed.

Install the Setting Bed

A carefully and accurately prepared setting bed is
a crucial part of working successfully with pavers.
Concrete paver manufacturers recommend using
concrete sand, which is coarser than other sands.
It drains more quickly and is less likely to spread
out over time. The setting bed should be 1 in.
thick, so you'll use 1-in. pipes to get the measurement right. Don't put down more setting
bed than you can cover with pavers before you
stop working for the day.

1. Lay two 1-in. pipes 4 ft. to 6 ft. apart and
perpendicular to the direction in which the
pavers will be installed. Because the patio is

level in this direction, the pipes should be too.
Place a level along the length of the pipes and
adjust them as necessary by hitting them with
a rubber mallet or gently with a metal hammer. Then span the pipes with a screed board,
place a level on the screed, and check the pitch,
which should be ¼ in. per ft. for this patio **A**.

2. When the pipes are positioned properly, put
a small amount of sand at the ends of each pipe
and along their lengths **B**. Then fill a portion
of the area between the pipes with sand and
rake it out roughly so that it is just above the
top of the pipes. Do not move the pipes.

3. Pull the screed along the tops of the pipes
using a side-to-side motion to create the

smooth surface . If you come to the end of a pipe before you come to the edge of the patio, you'll need to move the pipe so you can continue adding sand to the correct depth. Gently slide the pipes in the sand until just a few inches remain in the bed. Then continue adding sand and screeding until you reach the ends of the pipes again or the end of the patio.

4. After the first section is complete, slide or gently lift out one pipe from the screeded setting bed and place it 4 ft. to 6 ft. from the remaining pipe. Level this pipe, anchor it with sand, and screed as before .

5. After you remove the pipes, fill in the voids they left with sand and trowel them smooth, as

shown in **E**. Do only what you can comfortably reach from the base without disturbing the setting bed. Fill in the rest as you install the concrete pavers. When you have put down as much setting bed as you can cover in a day, stop and install the pavers.

Install the Concrete Pavers

After a portion of the setting bed is in place, it's time to install the pavers. To keep the pattern running true, you must lay the pavers along a straight line. It's also important to spend extra time laying the first few rows of pavers to make sure that you begin accurately. Errors here can compound themselves later on.

The pattern used in this patio is called the "I" pattern. It's a simple but interesting pattern that utilizes just two sizes of pavers—6 in. by 6 in. and 6 in. by 9 in. (see the drawing on p. 85).

Install the first section of pavers

1. At the approximate center of the patio and perpendicular to the width, install two stakes the length of the patio but outside of the perimeter. Pull a string taut between them, about 1 in. above the surface of the sand **A**. Use this string to keep the pavers running straight.

(see the drawing on p. 85).

WHAT CAN GO WRONG

As you pull the screed, excess sand will build up in front of it. It is harder to screed against the weight of the excess sand, and if too much sand builds up it can spill over the top of the screed and you'll have to rescreed. So from time to time, stop screeding and remove the excess with your hands or a trowel.

PRO TIP

To prevent your stockpile of bedding sand from drying out, getting too wet from rain, or being contaminated with twigs and leaves, cover it with a tarp.

PRO TIP

Installing pavers is much faster when you have someone "feeding" you pavers—carrying them from the cubes and stacking them within arm's length.

A

B

C

Selecting Pavers

VARIATIONS IN COLOR SHADES ARE INHERENT in concrete pavers, and different cubes of pavers may contain a dominant shade. Unless there is a specific reason to group shades together, it's usually more visually appealing to distribute the various shades throughout the patio. To avoid color "blotches," try these three things:

• As you lay pavers in one area, always take from different cubes.

• As you pick from a cube, don't remove one layer across the top completely. Instead, work through the cube vertically—by removing entire stacks—or diagonally, choosing from multiple stacks.

• As you work, stand back and check for color variations. You can replace pavers as needed to create an even look.

2. On one side of the string line, begin to lay the pattern (see the sidebar on the facing page). Because of the free-form shape of this patio, the exact outside edge of the patio will be determined after the pavers have been installed. That means the outermost pavers are installed beyond the edge of the finished patio, which is indicated by the pin flags. Later, after the finished edge is cut, any extra pavers are removed and used elsewhere in the patio.

3. Install additional pavers along the bottom of the patio until you reach the edge, as shown in **B** (see the sidebar on the facing page). Then move back to the string and continue with the pattern. When working next to the string, make sure that no pavers touch it and push it out of alignment. Temporarily leave out any pavers that would cross the string **C**. They will be installed as the second side is done.

After you have installed enough pavers, you can work from on top of the pavers, but move carefully so that you don't disturb the pavers you've already installed. It's actually a good idea to work from a piece of plywood because you don't have to be as careful and it provides a good surface on which to stack pavers **D**. As you approach the voids left by the pipes, fill them in with some additional sand and level it with a trowel.

4. Cover the setting bed completely with pavers on one side of the string. Remove the string, then install the pavers to cover the other side of the prepared setting bed. Replace the string before starting the next section of the setting bed, wrapping one end around a paver and setting on top of the installed pavers. As you near the intersection with the walkway, you can stop work on the patio or start on the walkway.

Connect the walkway

Installing a walkway that connects the patio with another feature like the screened porch shown

D

WHAT CAN GO WRONG

Never walk on the pavers within about 1 ft. of the patio edge because that can cause the sand to collapse at the edges. If this does happen, remove all the affected pavers until you reach undisturbed sand, reshape the setting bed, and replace the pavers.

I-Pattern Installation

YOU'LL SEE A CAPITAL "I" FORMED within this pattern (see the drawing below right). Here's how to install it.

Begin at the string and lay two pavers—1 and 2—with the long edge parallel to the string. Then lay pavers 3, 4, and 5. Notice how paver 4 projects 3 in., or one-third its length, beyond 3 and 5.

It's better to build the pattern across before building up, so next install paver 6,

making it flush with the right side of paver 3, and then lay 7, 8, 9, and 10. Continue across with pavers 11 through 16. So that you don't move a paver that's already installed, try to avoid having to slip a paver inside three sides. That's why paver 16 is installed before 17.

Once it's started, the pattern will continue to develop naturally.

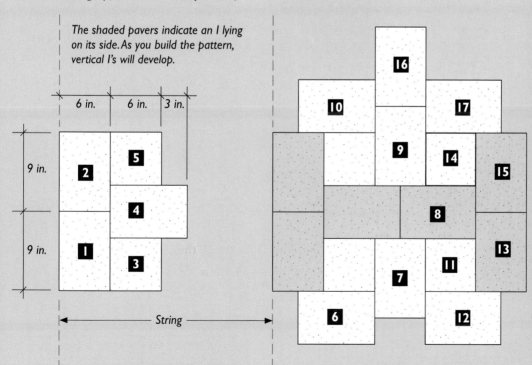

The shaded pavers indicate an I lying on its side. As you build the pattern, vertical I's will develop.

here is merely a matter of extending the paver pattern along the length of the walkway. Even though this walkway curves, the pattern does not. It continues to run in the same direction. The curve is created by cutting the edges of the pavers after they are installed.

1. Temporarily put the screeding pipes along the walkway to determine how many bedding installation sections will be needed. This project required two, with the break at the curve.

2. Beginning at the steps, lay two 1-in. pipes parallel to the length of the walkway and level them across the width of the stairs. If your walkway is long or requires a few days to complete, begin installing the setting bed at the patio and work toward the steps. To double-

check that the setting bed is at the correct height, place a paver on top of the pipe near the steps and measure the riser height **E**. Be sure to account for the ⅜ in. of settling.

3. Install the first setting bed section as before (see p. 82).

4. Remove and reposition both pipes for the next setting bed section **F**. To check the height of the base where the walkway intersects the patio, place a paver on top of the pipes to see if the tops of the walkway and patio pavers are in the same plane **G**. Adjust the pipes as needed to achieve this alignment. Install the rest of the setting bed.

5. Returning to the patio, continue laying the pavers, extending the pattern up the walkway **H**.

6. For the most efficient use of your materials, leave a portion of the walk and patio unfinished and start shaping the edge now. That way you'll

E

F

G

find out which pavers are extra (see p. 88), and
you can use them in the remaining installation.
If you complete the paver installation and then
cut the edge, you'll end up with a lot of extra
pavers and pieces.

Shape the Edge

The outside edge of a patio or walkway is typically finished with a border course. A soldier
course of 6-in. by 9-in. pavers is used here.

Cut the pavers

1. Lay the soldier pavers around the perimeter
of the previously installed portions of the patio
and walkway **A**. The pavers will not fit tight,
edge to edge, on the curves. Take your time and
adjust the shape of the curves to please your eye.

2. Using a gas-powered cut-off saw, outline the
inside edge of the soldier course by scoring the
surface of the pavers **B**, **C**. Although a scored
line is more permanent than a pencil line, use a
pencil or marking crayon if you will be using
a guillotine cutter or circular saw, or if it makes
you feel more comfortable.

3. Cut the pavers. Although you can cut them in place, it's better to remove them one by one and cut them individually. Remove each paver by carefully putting your fingers under it and gently lifting straight up without disturbing the setting bed. Or, if the edges are exposed, you can grab them and lift the paver out. Place the paver on level, clear ground and cut it (see p. 148 for a way to secure small pavers when cutting).

4. Continue with this process until the entire edge of the prepared portion of the patio and walkway have been cut **D**. Save the cut pieces because you may be able to use them as you finish the paver installation.

Cut-to-Fit Edges

WHERE THE PATIO OR WALKWAY MEETS A FIXED EDGE (for example, the stairs at the screened porch), you need to measure the size of each individual piece to get the right fit.

To get an accurate measurement, align your tape measure or framing square with the joints in the pavers **A**. Then cut and install the individual pieces **B**.

Install the soldier course

Although it's not crucial, it usually makes sense to start the border course at a defined point, such as a corner. This soldier course was begun at the intersection of two curves. And because it seemed more visually pleasing, the inside curve continues through the soldier course to the outside edge. Straight-run borders are relatively simple to put down—one soldier paver is butted directly up against the next. However, to get tight joints between pavers installed on curves, you must do some cutting.

1. Place a paver on one side of the intersection of the two curves, and mark it with an extension of the intersecting curve. This can be done either freehand or by using a piece of the edge restraint. Cut the paver and put it back in place **E**.

2. To hold this cut paver in place, install a few soldier-course pavers next to it. Then position the first inside curve paver so that the joint of the adjacent soldier will not line up with the joint between the patio and the outside soldier course. Mark it by extending the outside curve, cut it, and put it in place. Then lay out the soldiers adjacent to the paver you just cut **F**.

3. The spaces between soldiers installed along a curve will open at the inside for inside curves or at the outside for outside curves **G**. You can install these soldiers along a curve without cutting them, but that leaves large spaces that have an unfinished look and can compromise the structural integrity of the border course. To create a tight joint, place a straightedge—a small torpedo level works well—over the joint

Cutting soldier-course pavers installed along a curve as shown in the photos above requires cutting both sides of each paver. Although this takes extra time, it is time well spent because it creates symmetrically shaped soldiers. The alternative, cutting only one side of each paver, creates a paver that has one angled edge and one straight edge. This can look out of balance, particularly when the joint is wide and a relatively large piece is cut off of one side.

between two soldiers and mark both sides **H**, **I**. Remove both pavers, cut them, and put them back in place **J**.

4. As you work, smooth any portion of the setting bed that might have been disturbed when removing the soldier pavers, then install the soldier course. Continue installing the soldier course until the prepared section of patio is done.

Install the edge restraint

Before moving on to install the next section of setting bed and pavers, install the edge restraint. The edge restraint locks the soldier course and

the bedding sand in place. It must be installed directly on top of the base, not the setting bed.

1. Using the edge of a trowel, carefully cut away the bedding sand right up to the edge of the pavers, as shown in **K**.

2. Pull the edge of the restraint tightly up against the pavers and nail it securely in place **L**. Edge restraints are flexible and easily conform to curves.

After installing the edge restraint, continue the layout as before, alternating the installation of the setting bed, pavers, and soldier courses, until the patio and walkway are finished.

Compact the Pavers and Fill the Joints

To create the interlocking bond that holds concrete and brick pavers, they must be compacted with a mechanical plate compactor. As the pavers are compacted, they settle into the setting bed and sand works its way up between the pavers, locking them in place.

1. Sweep the surface clean of any debris, then spread a thin layer of bedding sand evenly over the pavers. This sand will protect the paver from being abraded by the compactor as it runs over the surface. Adjust the speed of the compactor so that it runs at a high vibration and at low amplitude (up and down motion) to avoid putting extra stress on the pavers.

2. Start at one edge and compact around the perimeter. Then, working back and forth and overlapping each pass 4 in. to 6 in., compact the entire surface. Turn 90 degrees and repeat the process. Make two or three passes at 90 degrees and be sure that each paver is compacted at least three times. (See the drawing on p. 38.)

3. Fill the joints with polymeric sand. Following the manufacturer's directions, spread some polymeric sand over the stones and sweep it into the joints until they are filled to the top **A**. Remove any excess sand and, beginning at the higher area near the house, wet the pavers and joints with a light spray of water **B**. Before walking on the patio and walkway, let the sand cure completely, which may take up to 24 hours depending on conditions.

A

B

(See the drawing on p. 38.)

PRO TIP

It's easier to install the edge restraint if you're on top of the pavers, but be careful not to disturb the border course. Work from on top of a piece of plywood to minimize the disturbance.

TRADE SECRET

If the sand is so dry that it slides out from under the pavers when you cut the edge of the setting bed, wet the pavers slightly so that the water gently drips through the joints and moistens the sand. If that approach doesn't work, install the edge restraint, then remove the pavers, put down additional sand, and reinstall them.

DINE IN STYLE

When it comes to creating new outdoor living space, patios designed for dining and grilling are at the top of many homeowners' wish lists. A patio just outside the dining room with a built-in grill fulfills that wish. An easy-access location means it gets lots of use. For steeply sloped lawns, a patio built on a retaining wall brings it closer to the home's living level and makes good use of the backyard.

This patio is paved with five sizes of regular bluestone flagging, installed in a random pattern. Cut bluestone is relatively smooth and uniform, so it provides an even surface for tables and chairs. A 16-in.-high wall, a vertical extension of the retaining wall, encircles the patio. A gas grill built into the western side and generous steps to the lawn complete this striking patio. ▶ ▶ ▶

Prepare the Site

The ground surrounding a newly constructed house can look more like a demolition zone than a residence, making it hard to visualize a finished landscape. However, one of the advantages of building a raised patio in these situations is that it's relatively easy to adjust the height of the final finished grade—the lawn—to match the layout of any stairs. This means that rather than changing the pitch of the steps, you can choose a rise-and-run relationship that's most comfortable.

If you're building your patio on an existing lawn area, you must excavate and remove the topsoil and replace it with an appropriate base material, like crushed gravel (see pp. 34–37 for more on excavation and base construction). During this process, you may be able to make small adjustments to the surrounding finish grade.

With new construction, the initial preparation takes place as the site is backfilled. To guard against future settling, it's important to make sure that the backfill material underneath the patio is extremely well compacted. While heavy equipment, typically a bulldozer, can do most of the job, the area adjacent to the foundation will need to be done with a plate compactor.

Before the backfilling begins, roughly mark out the general area of the patio. Then as the excavating contractor compacts the patio area with the bulldozer, simultaneously use a mechanical plate compactor to compact the area closest to the foundation in lifts, or increments, of 3 in. to 4 in.

Establish Heights and Final Layout

Patios are built from the bottom up, but when they are next to a house, they are laid out from the top down so that you set the correct distance from the house to the patio. The crucial height dimensions are the top of the patio and the top of the patio base.

Find the patio height

1. Establish the top of the patio by measuring down from the inside finish floor the desired distance—in this case one riser, or 7 in.—and make a mark on the foundation **A**. Then use a level to transfer that mark to a corner of the foundation **B**. These marks represent the top of the patio.

A

9 ft.

North

42 in.

2 ft.

14 in.

14 in.

Back edge
of top tread

6 ft.

Bluestone
flagging

C

8 ft. 8 in.

R

1 ft. 6 in.

10 ft. 5 in.

Grill

B

Sitting room

10 ft.

8 ft.

8 ft.

9 ft. 4 in.

Edge of base

1 ft. 4 in.

Dining room

5 ft.

B

PRO TIP

The amount that ground slopes can be deceiving. Before you start, use a line level to determine if—and how much—your site slopes.

2. You need to determine the height of the patio base. This bluestone flagging is a uniform thickness (1 in.) and are installed on a 1-in. stone-dust setting bed. Measure down from the marks you made in step 1 the total thickness of the stone and setting bed—2 in. in our example —and make a mark **C**.

3. Hold a chalkline on the lower mark you just made on the corner, pull it along the entire length of the wall—aligning it with the mark below the original mark—and snap a line **D**. This level line represents the top of the base. Alternately, you can use a string and line level to create this level line. If the patio touches more than one wall, be sure to mark the correct pitch on those adjacent walls (see p. 33 for more information on determining pitch).

Lay out the patio

1. Once the crucial patio heights are established, lay out the perimeter of the patio. The edge of this patio is defined by a circular wall that's approximately 16 in. wide at the top. Although the finished patio is defined by the inside of the wall, the layout begins by locating the outside of the wall. To do this, locate the center of the circle, which is done first on paper by trial and error and then transferred on site. The goal is to have a radius long enough to encompass the west corner of the dining room and also incorporate the south corner of the sitting room.

2. The radius is centered on the sliding glass door. The distance from the door to the center point was determined first on paper by adjusting the length of the radius until the desired lengths—8 ft. to stake R and a 9-ft. 4-in. radius for this project—were achieved. This can also be done directly on site by measuring with a tape measure and trying different distances until the correct one is found.

3. The center of the stone wall lines up with the corner of the house. Figuring in the width of the wall at the top—16 in.—means that the outside of the wall at the top is 10 ft. from the center point. But because retaining walls slope inward from the base, the radius is wider at the

information on pitches on p. 33). Over its 17-ft. length, the patio slopes down about $4\frac{1}{4}$ in. ($\frac{1}{4}$ in. x 17 ft.). The retaining-wall section of the wall is built to the height of the base and must also pitch. To mark the pitch, use a line level to transfer the height of the base at the foundation (the original mark) to each stake. Then, on stake A, measure down the amount of the pitch—$4\frac{1}{4}$ in.—and make a mark; determine the perpendicular distance from the house wall to stakes B and C, 8 ft. here, and measure down the correct distance, or 2 in. for this project.

Lay out the steps

A set of steps made of dry-stone risers and bluestone treads provides easy access to the surrounding lawn. With 6-in. risers and 14-in.-deep treads, these steps are integrated into the retaining wall (see the drawing on p. 95). That means they must be built at the same time. The steps begin 18 in. out from the sitting room corner and are 6 ft. wide. The top tread is actually part of the patio as well as the steps.

1. To establish the height of the stair base, on stake C measure down the total rise and mark the number of risers required to reach the adjacent ground. This project has an 18-in. total rise, which requires three 6-in. risers.

2. Where the steps will be constructed, roughly lay out an area large enough to include the steps and retaining wall. The exact position and relationship/angle of the steps to the wall will be determined by eye as the wall is built.

bottom of the wall (see the drawing on p. 47). The wall is approximately 5 ft. high from the base of the retaining wall to the top of the freestanding wall and pitches in about 1 in. per ft., or a total of 5 in. To account for this "batter," the radius at the bottom of the wall is 10 ft. 5 in. Using a tape measure, swing a 10-ft. 5-in. arc while simultaneously spray-painting a line **E**. Alternately, you can mark the arc with a stick and paint the line afterward.

4. After the outside of the wall has been painted, install three stakes, A, B, and C, around the perimeter and aligned with the radius point (see the drawing on p. 95). Put the stakes 2 in. to 3 in. out from the line so that they don't interfere with the construction of the wall.

5. This patio, and its base, has a 2 percent ($\frac{1}{4}$-in. per ft.) pitch away from the house (see

TRADE SECRET

You might find the thought of building a level patio on sloping ground somewhat daunting. If you have a sloping site, don't panic—many homes do. Even patios on level sites must be raised because the first floors of most houses are 18 in. or more above the ground. The same techniques— retaining walls, fill, and steps—are used to deal with slopes and on-level sites to raise patios closer to floor level.

Install the Base Material

Because the rough grade of this project was significantly below the planned height of the patio, the retaining wall was built in conjunction with the installation of the base. For this project, the base consists of two parts—a gravel subbase and a crushed, recycled base material (hard pack) about 6 in. thick. The gravel is used to level the rough grade, whereas the recycled material compacts better than gravel.

1. Place geotextile fabric on the ground around the perimeter of the wall. The fabric can be cut with shears to match the curve. Then lay the first few courses of the wall (see "Build the dry-stone" on p. 46). Put ¾-in. crushed stone behind the wall, on top of the geotextile fabric **A**.

2. Fill the area inside the wall with gravel, rake the gravel out smooth, and compact it with a plate compactor. The gravel should be installed in small lifts, 3 in. to 4 in. thick. Use a hand tamper to compact the areas near the foundation and wall.

3. Build the wall about 6 in. higher, and pull the filter fabric up the inside of the wall. Fill behind the wall with additional gravel. Rake and compact as before. Repeat this process until the gravel subbase is about 6 in. below the base line **B**.

4. Continue building the wall but now filling behind it with the base material, which you also compact. Keep going until the wall and base reach the top of the base line, or 2 in. below the top of the patio **C**. You can pull strings between the stakes to guide you to the proper height or use a builder's sight level **D**.

Integrate the Steps

As the wall is constructed around to the east and approaches the location of the stairs, integrate the steps into the wall. (For more information on building steps, see p. 160.)

1. Compact a base area large enough to allow some shifting of the position of the steps.

2. Determine the location of the top tread. This is done by eye, using a string or straight-edge as a guide **A**. Once you're happy with the location, mark the back edge of the top tread with paint. Outline the steps with painted lines, making sure that they are square. To get a better sense of how the steps will build out, you can mark the location of the treads with paint.

3. Build the wall up to the height of the first riser, then build the riser. Fill the area behind the first riser with crushed stone, and put the

tread in place. Make sure it is level side to side and front to back, and that it's aligned with the mark on stake C **B**.

4. Continue to build the wall and steps until you reach the top of the patio **C**, **D**.

Install the Setting Bed

A carefully and accurately installed setting bed eliminates a lot of flagstone installation problems and creates a superior finished patio. To avoid disturbing the setting bed, this patio is finished section by section. A small area of setting bed material (stone dust was used for this project), is installed, followed by the bluestone. This process is repeated until the entire patio is completed. It's important not to put down more setting bed than you can cover with pavers before you stop working for the day. For more specific information about installing a setting bed for bluestone pavers, see pp. 63–66.

1. Use 1-in. pipes to create the proper thickness of the setting bed. At the house wall, place two pipes on the patio base, parallel to each other in the direction that the patio slopes. Check for the proper pitch by placing a level on the pipes. If necessary, strike the pipe with a rubber mallet or gently with a metal hammer until the correct pitch is achieved **A**. Then check for level across the two pipes and adjust as necessary.

2. To hold the pipes in position, cover the ends with bedding material. Then cover them slightly and fill the area between the pipes with setting material **B**.

3. Using a screed, level and smooth the setting material .

4. When you reach the end of the pipes, gently pull the pipes through the screeded setting bed, stopping when about 6 in. of the pipes are still embedded in the stone dust **D**. Repeat steps

1 through 3 until you've reached the end of the first section of patio.

5. As you finish this section, carefully place a small amount of bedding material into the voids left by the pipes and smooth it out with a small trowel. Only fill what you can comfortably reach—the rest is filled as you lay the

WHAT CAN GO WRONG

If there is too much material between the pipes, the excess is likely to crest over the top of the screed and spill backward onto the previously screeded section. When this happens, you will have to screed the area again. Having too little material can also be a problem. As you screed, if you notice a trough beginning to form, stop, push a little material from the unscreeded area into the low spot, and then continue screeding. With time and experience, you'll develop an eye for how much "is enough" and learn to fill in the correct amount.

1. Choose one of the larger-size stones—one that is big and heavy enough to provide a solid starting point but not so large that it is difficult to lift and maneuver. We installed an 18-in. by 18-in. stone first. While kneeling on a section of the base, place one edge of the stone against the foundation and gently lower it onto the setting bed.

2. Lay a few additional stones to begin the pattern, adjusting the spaces between them as needed. Use a small pry bar to move the stones side to side to make small adjustments.

3. Compact the stones into the setting bed either by stepping on them firmly or by tapping them with a rubber mallet. Then use a 4-ft. level or other straightedge to check the stones **A**. Some variation in height is unavoidable, but to provide a smooth surface for table and chair legs, try to keep differences to $\frac{1}{16}$ in. or less. (Keep in mind that if you are checking stones in the direction that the patio pitches, they will not be level, which is okay as long as you've got the pitch correct.) If a paver is too low or too high, gently lift it up, add or remove some setting-bed material, smooth it out with a trowel, and set the stone back in place.

4. Continue with the installation as outlined in steps 2 and 3 above. To ensure that the pattern and joints are running square to the wall, check from time to time in more than one location and as you add to the pattern. Using a square, pull a string at a right angle to the wall and sight along, or measure to, the joints **B**, **C**.

pavers—and don't fill the void where you need to replace a pipe to install an additional section of setting bed.

6. Install flagstones to cover the setting bed (see "Lay the Bluestone" below) before installing the next section of setting bed.

Lay the Bluestone

Once the first section of the setting bed is prepared, you're ready to begin installing the finish bluestone. This patio uses a completely random pattern with five sizes of stones: 1 ft. by 1 ft., 1 ft. by 2 ft., 18 in. by 18 in., 18 in. by 2 ft., and 2 ft. by 3 ft. A $\frac{1}{2}$-in. joint is left between the stones. A circular patio like the one shown here works well with a random pattern because it is flexible enough to accommodate curves and accept adjustments as needed.

A

B

C

Cut-Stone Paver Patterns

YOU ARE NOT RESTRICTED to a standard running bond pattern. Try creating your own pattern. Manufacturers and suppliers may also offer their own patterns and provide the number and sizes of stones required.

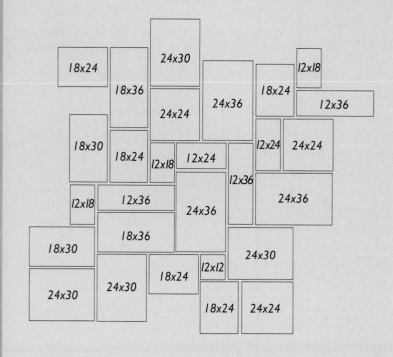

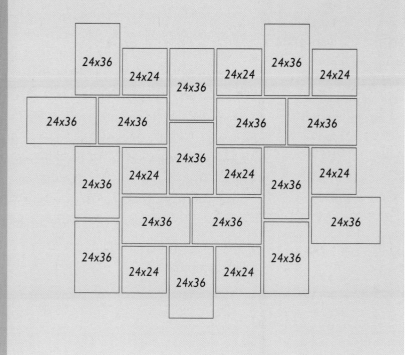

D

5. When you reach the edge of the patio or corner of the house, you must cut the edge pieces to fit. Measure the space for the stone **D**. Transfer the measurements to an appropriate-size piece, and cut the stone to size **E**. Lay the cut piece in place. Because the edges of this patio will be covered by the freestanding wall or are up against the foundation, there is no need for an edge restraint. If you're not planning to cover the edges with a freestanding wall, install an edge restraint now (see p. 72 for instructions).

E

Complete the Freestanding Wall

Before you fill the joints, complete the freestanding wall. This way you can easily replace a piece of bluestone if it gets broken or chipped while the wall is being built. (See p. 46 for more information on building walls.)

1. Locate the inside face of the wall. As you did in steps 4 and 5 on p. 97, find the center of the circular patio. From that point, swing an arc with a string or tape equal to the radius of the circle at the inside face of the wall— 8 ft. 8 in. (10 ft. – 1 ft. 4 in. [the width of the wall]) in this example—and mark it (see the photo on p. 92 and the drawing on p. 95).

2. Lay out the base course for the inside face, including the sections that are on either end

of the steps. Place crushed stone between the inside and outside pieces of the wall stones **A**.

3. Continue building the wall up toward the finished height—16 in. above the patio here. As you near the top of the wall, make sure the stones are level across the width of the wall. This is particularly important in the narrow freestanding section that flanks the steps **B**.

4. As you approach the location of the grill, build the wall to accommodate it. The outside of the wall goes behind the stove, where it is reduced in width to about 10 in., and the two returns, which have finished faces, extend out from the wall to encase the grill. The distance between the returns must be wide enough to accommodate the grill **C**.

PRO TIP

If you're planning a built-in grill, utility pipes and conduits can be hidden inside a portion of the wall.

WHAT CAN GO WRONG

As you build the free-standing portion of the wall, you might be tempted to work the stone on the patio surface. Yes, it can be time-consuming and tiresome to break and cut the stones on the ground and carry them to the wall, but even if the work area is protected with plywood, it's a bad idea to work directly on it. The heavy blows of a hammer on stone can compress the patio flagstones into the setting bed, or even break them. Trimming and breaking wall stone also creates a lot of small flying chips and pieces, which can end up in the joints and would have to be removed before the joints could be filled.

5. Install the capstones. Use a cut-off saw to make the cuts on the faces that butt against the wall **D**. If you don't have a cut-off saw, use a circular saw equipped with a diamond blade, or shape the faces with a stone hammer **E**. (See p. 47 for more information on installing caps.)

PRO TIP

Do not direct a stream of water directly at the joints. The force might be strong enough to force the stone dust out.

Fill the Joints

After the wall is completed, fill the joints. You can use stone dust, but the ½-in.-wide, 1-in.-thick joints in this patio are filled with a polymeric sand. Polymeric sand is available in a wide range of colors, it resists weed growth, and it doesn't wash away as stone dust can.

1. Inspect all the joints and remove any stray pieces of wall stone or excess dust. Then wet the entire patio with a hose to compact the stone dust. Before pouring out the polymeric sand, make sure the pavers are completely dry. It's all right if the setting bed is damp.

2. Following the manufacturer's directions, spread an appropriate amount of polymeric sand over the stones. Sweep the polymeric sand over the joints until they are filled to the top . Sweep any excess off of the surface, and make sure it is completely clean of all of the sand particles.

3. Beginning near the house and working in the direction of the pitch, gently spray the entire surface. This will wash away any remain-ing unseen particles and dust. Be careful not to wash the sand from between the joints. Manufacturers generally recommend wetting the sand again after 10 to 15 minutes, and it usually takes about 24 hours for it to com-pletely harden.

The finished patio is the perfect spot for dining.

FROM BLAND TO BEAUTIFUL

It's a common predicament—you want to welcome guests in an attractive way that reflects your personality and your home's style. However, the once-new concrete walk and patio have aged and become worn to the point that they lack character and have become, well, an eyesore. Addressing a walkway is straightforward, particularly if it is rebuilt in the same location, but you might consider widening the walkway, or at least its entrance, to make it more inviting. And enlarging a too-small patio can create valuable additional space and improve traffic patterns.

Most guests arriving at this home use the back walk/patio entrance. To update and improve it, the patio was enlarged by building a retaining wall, and the steps leading to the yard were relocated to be in line with the back door. Both the walkway and wall are constructed with mica schist and are interspersed with rounded "cobbles." The retaining wall extends above the patio to form a freestanding wall that acts as a guardrail and provides additional seating. ▶ ▶ ▶

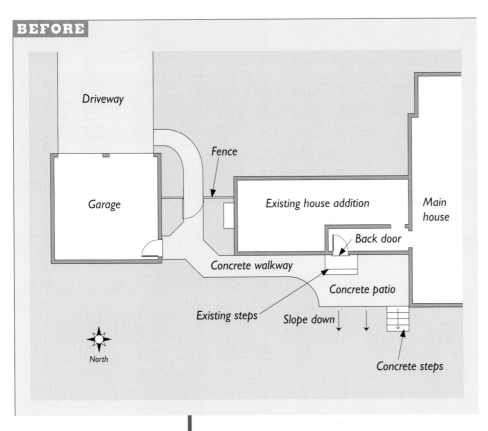

Driveway

Fence

Garage

Existing house addition

Main house

Back door

Concrete walkway

Concrete patio

Existing steps

Slope down

Concrete steps

North

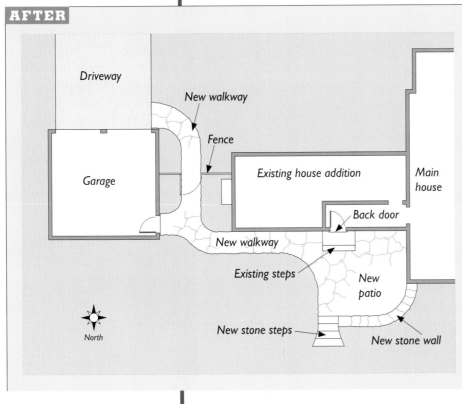

Driveway

New walkway

Fence

Garage

Existing house addition

Main house

Back door

New walkway

Existing steps

New patio

New stone steps

New stone wall

North

Prepare the Site

When you're replacing an existing patio or walkway in basically the same footprint, the site preparation consists mainly of demolition. The concrete for most walks and patios is installed in 4-ft. to 5-ft. sections, so it is relatively easy to remove without power tools.

1. Since it is much easier to break up concrete when it is raised above the ground, start by jamming the end of a large pry or digging bar under the edge of a section of concrete. Put a fulcrum—a piece of a 4x4 works well—under the bar and pry up the concrete slab. To hold it in place, slide two short pieces of 4x4 under each end of the slab **A**.

A

2. Using an 8-lb. sledgehammer, strike a series of successively harder blows parallel to the supported edge. Continue until the concrete breaks.

3. At right angles to the first break, strike the concrete until that piece breaks in half **B**. Break up the slab into pieces that can easily be removed with a hand truck. Repeat this process until all the concrete has been removed.

Establish Heights and Layout

The first task is to locate the top of the patio surface along the back wall. The existing stairs to the back door, which were not removed, are used to establish the height of the patio.

1. Measure the existing riser height—which is 7¾ in. in this example **A**. At the front of the stairs, the patio should be one-riser height below the first tread. Then calculate the total height of the stairs, 15½ in. (2 × 7¾ in.).

2. To shed water, this patio has a pitch of 2 percent, or ¼ in. over 12 in., away from the house. This means that at the back wall,

the patio will be higher than at the first riser. Measure how far the steps project out from the house—3 ft. 6 in.—and calculate the pitch for that distance (3.5 ft. × ¼ in./ft. = ⅞ in., rounded down to ¾ in.). To find the height of the patio at the back wall, deduct the amount of the pitch from the total height of the steps (15½ in. – ¾ in. = 14¾ in.). Install a stake, A, at the intersection of the back wall and stairs (see the drawing on p. 112). Measure down from the top step 14¾ in. and mark the stake with this top-of-the-patio measurement **B**.

3. Install another stake, B, at the intersection of the back and west walls. Using a line level, pull a string from the top-of-patio mark on stake A to stake B, make a level mark on stake B, and

see the drawing on p. 112

If the ground below the concrete is soft, the 4x4 fulcrum might compress into it. To regain your leverage, stack a second 4x4 on top of the first.

TRADE SECRET

Concrete slabs are often reinforced with a grid of welded wire. If your concrete doesn't break completely apart when it's hammered, that's probably the reason why. To create manageable pieces, the wire will have to be cut. You should be able to do this with a sharp, quick blow of the digging bar. If not, use a large pair of wire or bolt cutters.

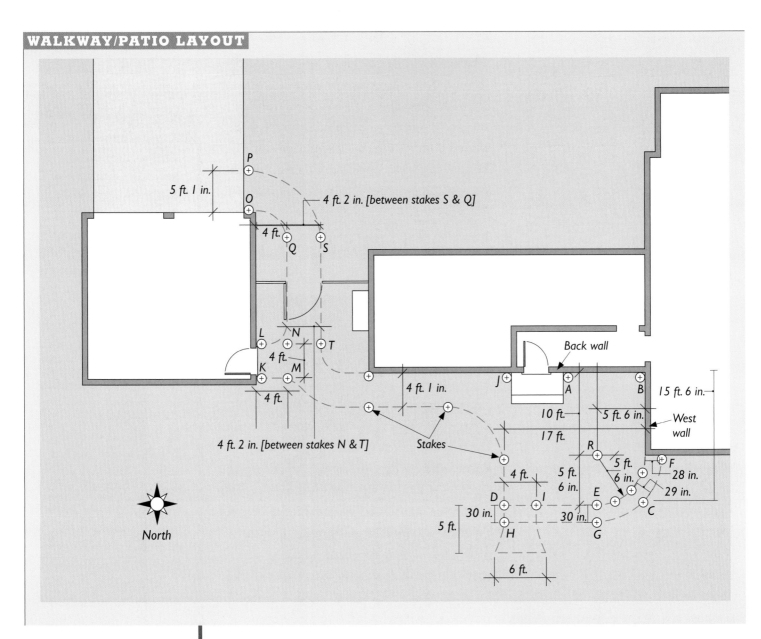

5 ft. 1 in.

4 ft. 2 in. [between stakes S & Q]

P

O

4 ft.

Q   S

Back wall

L   N

4 ft.

K   M   T

4 ft.

4 ft. 1 in.

J   A   B   15 ft. 6 in.

10 ft.   5 ft. 6 in.   West wall

17 ft.

4 ft. 2 in. [between stakes N & T]

Stakes

R   5 ft.   F

4 ft.   5 ft.   6 in.   28 in.

6 in.   E   29 in.

D   I   C

30 in.   30 in.

5 ft.   H   G

6 ft.

North

---

tie the string between the two **C**. The patio is level across the back wall.

4. Determine the amount the patio pitches from the back all the way to the front. Install a stake, C, in line with the west wall to represent the front of the patio—15 ft. 6 in. away from the back wall (see the drawing above). Using a line level, pull a string from stake B to stake C and mark the level line. Then calculate the total amount of pitch (¼ in./ft. × 15.5 ft. = 3⅞ in.,

C

rounded up to 4 in.). Measure down 4 in. from the level mark, mark the top of the patio, and tie a string from stake B to C .

5. The patio is level across the front. At the east end of the patio, install a stake, D, 17 ft. from stake C and 15 ft. 6 in. from the back wall. Pull a level line from the top-of-patio mark on stake C, and mark it on stake D .

6. Measure 5 ft. 6 in. from stake C and install stake E. This represents the point at which the curve, or radius, starts (see the drawing on the facing page).

Lay out the wall base

The next step is to lay out the stone wall base. The freestanding portion of the wall is 18 in. above the top of the patio and 24 in. wide at the top. However, because retaining walls slope inward from the base, the wall is wider at the bottom (see "Dry-Stone Wall Construction" on p. 47). The north side of the stone wall is 3 ft. high (from the base of the retaining wall to the top of the freestanding wall) and slopes in about 1 in. per ft., or a total of 3 in. To account for this "batter," the bottom of the wall is about 27 in. wide. As the slope of the ground rises as it nears the house, the wall gets narrower at the bottom, to about 26 in. wide halfway around the curve and 25 in. wide at the house wall.

1. Lay out the inside curved section of wall. The inside radius of the curve is 5 ft. 6 in., and the inside edge of the wall is aligned with the corner of the west wall (see the drawing on the facing page). Locate the center of the radius by measuring 5 ft. 6 in. from the inside corner along the back wall of the house. Then pull a tape out from this point parallel to, and the length of, the west wall, 10 ft. in this example. At the house corner, pull a tape out the length of the radius, 5 ft. 6 in. Where the two tapes cross, install a stake, R.

2. From stake R, swing a 5-ft. 6-in. arc with the tape and install three stakes that approximately divide the curve evenly. These stakes mark the inside of the wall and the outside edge of the patio.

3. Lay out the outside of the curve. For this step, the edge of the base, not the wall, is laid out. The wall base is about 3 in. wider than the bottom of the wall. At this point, the layout doesn't have to be precise. From stake E, measure out 30 in. and install stake G (see the drawing on p. 112). From the middle stake at the inside of the curve, measure out the width of the base, 29 in. at this point, and mark this spot with paint or a stake. (This point may coincide with stake C.) From the northwest corner, measure over 28 in. and install stake F. Then, using a measuring tape or your eye to guide you, complete the curve with a painted line.

Locate the walkway

Once the patio heights and layout are determined, locate the top of the walkway—which is largely determined by the existing grade and surface of the driveway—and the walkway width.

1. Install a stake, J, at the intersection of the east side of the existing steps and the back wall, and locate the top of the patio as you did in step 2 on p. 111 **F**.

2. At the side entrance to the garage, install two stakes, K and L, about 2 in. wider than the

walkway to account for the width of the base. Mark the height of the existing grade on them, which is the top of the walkway. Measure out 4 ft. from each side of the door, which is about 1 in. shy of the opening in the gate, install two stakes, M and N, and mark them with the top of the grade/patio.

3. Install two additional stakes, O and P, 5 ft. 1 in. apart where the walkway intersects the driveway. Mark the top of the walkway on them, which is the top of the driveway (see the drawing on p. 112).

4. Determine the shape of the curve at the driveway either by eye or with a garden hose. Install stake Q 4 ft. from the garage wall where the curve ends and stake S 4 ft. 2 in. from stake Q. Install stake T 4 ft. 2 in. from stake N. Install other stakes at any critical points, again at least 1 in. wider than the walk, such as opposite the corner of the house and where the straight sections of walkway intersect the existing curves (see the drawing on p. 112). Mark these stakes with the top of the walkway and existing grade, which pitches away from the house.

5. Pull strings between the stakes. These strings indicate the width of the walkway base and set the top of the walkway and guide the installation stone flagging **G**.

6. Lay out the area for the steps, which project 5 ft. from stake D and are 6 ft. wide at the beginning (see the drawing on p. 112).

F

Build the Stone Wall and Steps

To bring the ground at the front end of the patio to the proper height, a stone retaining wall is built. The new set of steps leading from the patio to the backyard is incorporated into the east end of the wall. Like the patio, the wall and the steps are constructed with mica schist.

1. Excavate the base area for the wall and steps. The exact depth varies with climate and soil type, but as a general rule remove from 6 in. to 12 in. of earth. As you excavate the curve, check the width by measuring from the stakes at the inside of the curve.

2. Lay geotextile fabric in the excavated areas, and install a well-draining base material, such as crushed gravel or stone, over the filter fabric. Three-quarter-inch trap rock was used here **A**.

Build the steps

Because they extend beyond the wall, construct the first few steps before starting the wall. (For more information on building steps, see p. 51 and p. 157.) These steps have a total rise of 30 in. (five risers of 6 in. each) and a total run of 5 ft. (four treads at 15 in. each). The second and succeeding risers are constructed on top of the treads, so the treads must be 2 in. to 4 in. deeper than the desired finish tread size.

1. To set the width of the top of the stairs, measure in 4 ft. from stake D and install stake I (see the drawing on p. 112).

2. Locate the position of the first riser, which is 5 ft. from the inside of the wall in this example. Build the first riser to the width of the first step, which is 6 ft. The height of the riser is the rise (6 in.) less the thickness of the tread.

see p. 51 and p. 157.

see the drawing on p. 112

3. Install the first tread on top of the first riser **B**. These steps narrow from 6 ft. to 4 ft. as they approach the top of the patio, with the first tread tapering the most. You can adjust the taper to suit your eye.

4. Build the second riser on top of the first tread at the proper tread depth, 15 in. here, and install the second tread. If you want the treads to overhang the riser, 1 in. for example, position the riser 16 in. deep instead. Do the same with the third riser and tread. The third tread intersects the wall, so you need to stop building the steps and start building the wall.

Build the wall

Start building the wall where it intersects the steps and work around toward the west wall. Before you begin, replace the guide string. Remember, about 3 in. in from the guide string denotes the width of the wall at the base, and as the wall is built taller, it will slope farther away from the string. (For additional information on building walls, see p. 44.)

1. Lay out a section of the base course of stones, securely bedding them in the trap-rock base. Fill in behind the stones with trap rock.

2. Add additional courses of stone, building the retaining wall until it is just above the third tread **C**. Continue to fill behind the stones with trap rock. (Alternately, you can lay out the entire base course before building additional courses.)

3. Because it is integrated into the wall, build the fourth riser, extending it into the wall, and install the fourth tread.

4. Continue building the wall **D**. As you proceed, check the height of the retaining wall with the guide string between stakes C and D.

E

F

(As the wall gets higher it might interfere with that string, so it's a good idea to transfer the top-of-patio mark to stakes E and I.)

5. When the retaining wall portion is about 3 in. below the top of the patio, start building the inside face of the freestanding wall. Lay out the base stones, add additional courses, and fill in between the inside and outside courses with trap rock **E**.

6. When the entire freestanding wall is above the plane of the top of the patio, install the patio's stone-dust setting bed (see "Install the Base and Setting Bed" on this page). Then install the last riser and tread, which are in line with the inside of the wall. Complete the wall by adding the capstones **F**.

Install the Base and Setting Bed

Crushed gravel is typically used for the base, and we got lucky for this project. The original concrete slab patio and walkway were installed on compacted gravel, which is also suitable for installing the new stone-flagging patio's base. If you're building over a lawn or other unprepared surface, you need to remove the soil containing organic material and install a proper base. (See p. 37 for more information on installing a base.)

After the base is set, install the setting bed. Stone dust was used for this setting bed.

1. Because the average thickness of the new stone is about 2 in. and the concrete slab that was removed was 4 in. thick, 2 in. of setting-bed material was needed to make up the difference and bring the patio stones to the proper height. Distribute stone dust over the gravel, and rake it to a relatively uniform thickness approximately 2 in. below the strings. The thickness of setting beds for rough stone does not have to be precise **A**.

2. Compact the stone dust. A 2-in.-thick layer of stone dust can be compacted by hand **B**,

A

WHAT CAN GO WRONG

It can be difficult to push a wheelbarrow or hand truck through a stone-dust setting bed. If you have to transport your patio stones through an area where you plan to install a setting bed, install the setting bed after you've moved the stones you need.

PRO TIP

Natural patio stone varies in thickness. Before you begin the setting bed, measure a representative sample of your stones to get a sense of their average thickness.

PRO TIP

To avoid hitting the strings while the base and setting bed are being compacted, temporarily remove them from the stakes. Put them back to take measurements.

TRADE SECRET

Before you begin, spread out the patio stones so that you can get a sense of the range of shapes, sizes, and color variation. Unless there is a specific design theme, it's generally best to aim for an even variation of sizes and color throughout the patio.

but thicker layers should be compacted with a mechanical compactor. Base and bedding materials compact more effectively when they are moist. If necessary, moisten the stone dust with a light spray of water before compacting. During the installation, the setting bed will be disturbed, but that's okay.

3. Following steps 1 and 2, install the setting bed for the walkway.

Install the Patio and Walkway Stone

With the steps and stone wall complete, install the patio stones. Laying irregularly shaped flagging is akin to building a large mosaic. Creating an attractive finished product requires two distinct skills: the ability to focus in on each individual stone, while at the same time paying attention to the big picture—the overall design. Start the patio at the back or far corner and work toward the front and the walkway.

Install the first stones

1. To install a stone, move it into position next to the wall and/or the adjacent stones and decide which edge to shape first. When installing a stone next to a straight surface, shape that edge first. Determine how much of the stone has to be removed **A**. Using a straightedge and a marking crayon or thick pencil, draw a trim line on the stone **B**.

2. Pull the stone away from the wall and begin to trim it to the line. Start with a 3-lb. sledgehammer, and as you near the line, finish with a lighter-weight mason's or stone hammer **C**, **D**. Slide the stone to the wall from time to time to check the fit.

C

E

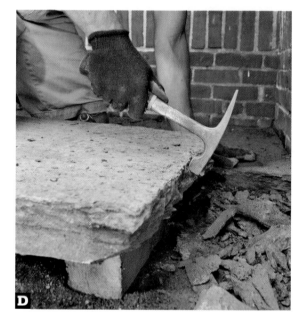

D

F

Fine-tune the setting bed

Once a stone is ready to be installed, the setting bed directly beneath it has to be fine-tuned before the stone is moved into its final position.

1. Remove the large waste pieces of stone by hand and rake away the smaller ones. Rake the area smooth and compact it **G**.

2. Check that the setting bed is at the correct height. Measure the thickness of the stone you're installing and the distance from the top of the previously installed stone to the setting bed **H**, **I**. These two measurements

3. When you're done trimming the first side of the stone, slide it against the wall (or an edge of a previously installed stone), overlapping the adjacent stone. Using the edge of the new stone as a guide, mark the installed stone **E**. It's also possible to trim the new stone to fit instead.

4. Use the back of the mason's hammer or your hand to dig away enough setting bed to expose the edge of the stone **F**. Then trim the stone as described in step 2.

PRO TIP

Patio stones are typically large and heavy. To minimize the amount they are moved, it is best to shape them at or near their final location.

TRADE SECRET

While shaping patio stones, support them slightly above the ground with some type of blocking, such as two 4x4s. As a stone is worked, it is frequently moved back and forth to check the fit. Not only do stones slide more easily on blocking, but this technique also minimizes the disturbance to the setting bed and makes it easier to shape the stone. The entire edge of a raised stone is visible, and as the wasted pieces of stone are broken off, they fall to the ground and out of the way.

should be equal. If they aren't, adjust the setting bed to accommodate the difference, either by removing or adding material.

3. When the setting bed is prepared, lower the stone and slide it into position. To "bed" the stone, place a sturdy piece of wood, such as a 4x4, on top of the stone, and firmly tamp the stone with a heavy bar **J**. Be careful not too use too much force or you could crack the stone.

4. When a stone is in its final position, stand back, assess the situation, and determine which stone to install next.

Adding Cobbles

AS AN ADDITIONAL DESIGN ELEMENT, cobbles can be added to a patio or walkway. These small, rounded stones provide visual intrigue, contrasting sharply with the large, flat pieces of flagging. You can use one cobble, or group two or more together. To install a cobble, first find one that roughly matches the size and shape of the hole. Next, trace the outline of the cobble on the patio stones and trim to accept the cobble. Then remove or add enough of the setting-bed material so that the cobble sits a little "proud" of, or above, the surface of the patio stones. Lay a sturdy piece of wood across the cobble, and use a 3-lb. sledgehammer to hammer the cobble flush with the surrounding stones.

Install the additional stones

As you work, it's easier if you only have to fit two stones to each other. Inevitably, however, there are times when you'll encounter a three-sided fit. Here's how to approach this situation.

1. Square off the innermost part of the adjacent stone. Draw a trim line on this stone **K**. Because a new stone will be fitted to this one, the line can be drawn freehand. (You can also do away with the line altogether and use your eye as a guide.) Trim the stone to this line.

2. Trim the other two sides as you did the first stone, to create a roughly rectangular shape.

3. Find a stone that is approximately the correct size and shape, and trim it to fit in the newly created space. As you work this final stone, you can fine-tune the stones that are already in place to make a perfect fit **L**.

4. As you continue to install the patio stones, don't forget to verify that the patio is running level across the back **M**. You also need to be sure it is pitching properly toward the front. Use a level or a string tied to the proper mark at a stake at the front of the patio to confirm the pitch. If you use a level, at 2 percent over 4 ft. the patio should drop about 1 in.

5. Continue to install the stones, working toward the front of the patio and the wall, as well as along the walkway. The last stones that butt against the wall can be scribed freehand **N**.

6. At the edges of the patio and walkway that are not defined by walls, shape the stones in place. This approach ensures that the edges of each stone line up perfectly with the adjacent stone. These cuts should follow a line drawn on the stones—don't go by eye alone. You can use a string as a guide for straight lines, and form curves freehand or use a flexible piece of wood, plastic, or other material **O**.

L

M

Fill the Joints

When all of the stones have been installed, fill the joints with stone dust. Spread a thin layer of the dust over the patio and walkway and sweep it into the cracks. Remove the excess, and then to compact it, wet the entire surface with a hose. Repeat as necessary until the cracks are completely filled. If, over time, you notice additional settling, install additional stone dust.

DISCOVER YOUR FRONT DOOR

When it comes to homes constructed over the last several decades, it seems that our love affair with the automobile has led us to ignore a once prominent feature–the front door. Driveways and garages have shifted our focus and, no longer the center of attention, the front door is often treated as a second-class citizen. While you may be able to see it, access to the front door might be obscured by overgrown plantings and can appear marooned behind a green sea of lawn. Additionally, front doors are often burdened with undersized and unattractive concrete steps.

Luckily, breathing new life into your front door can be relatively straightforward. Begin by creating a new walkway, positioning it so that it's easily visible to guests and directs your attention toward the front door. Then, build a welcoming set of steps and generous landing that make your guests feel safe and emphasize the importance of the front door. ▶ ▶ ▶

BEFORE

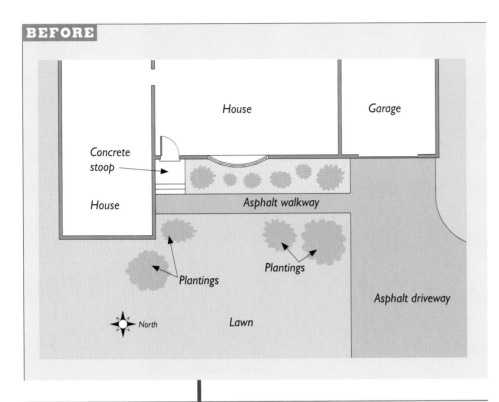

House

Garage

Concrete stoop

House

Asphalt walkway

Plantings

Plantings

Asphalt driveway

North

Lawn

AFTER

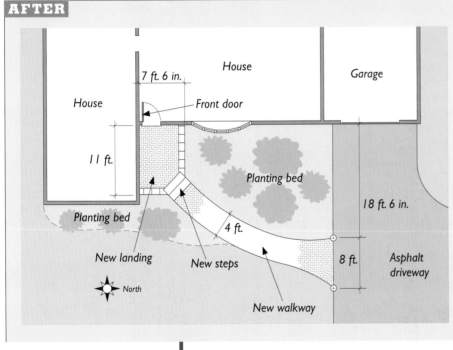

7 ft. 6 in.

House

Garage

House

Front door

11 ft.

Planting bed

18 ft. 6 in.

Planting bed

New landing

New steps

4 ft.

8 ft.

Asphalt driveway

North

New walkway

Uninviting and ordinary, the original landing and walkway needed an update.

Initial Layout

Do an initial layout of the project before doing any other work. This walkway is 4 ft. wide and leads to a landing that's 7 ft. 6 in. by 11 ft. The landing created by a concrete-block retaining wall is one step below the first floor and is covered with concrete pavers. The landing pitches away from the front door about ¼ in. per ft. to shed water (see p. 33). Two 6-in. risers bridge the distance from the top of the walkway to the landing.

Initial landing layout

The first task is to locate the position of the landing and the retaining wall, and determine the landing height.

1. Find the approximate location of the landing and steps. Mark the width and length of the new landing on the foundation, 7 ft. 6 in. and 11 ft., respectively. Establish the edges of the landing and placement of the steps as described on p. 130, and install stakes B, C, and D. Then install stakes E and F (see the top drawing on the facing page). For the purposes of this initial layout and subsequent site excavation, the stake placement doesn't have to be precise. Do not offset the stakes 3 in., as shown in the drawing.

2. Find the difference between the height of the finish grade at the steps—which is also the height of the walkway—and the first floor. Pull a line level from the first floor, and mark stake D with the first-floor height (see the drawing below). You can also use a builder's sight level. Then measure the distance from that mark to the finish grade. Also, at this time, measure the distance from the first floor to the finish grade at the house.

3. Calculate how many steps/risers will be needed to bridge the distance from finish grade/top of walkway to the first floor. Deduct the amount that the patio pitches from the total rise (22 in. − 2¾ in. = 19¼ in. for this project). Subtract the total rise of the steps from this number (19¼ in. − 12 in. = 7¼ in.). This

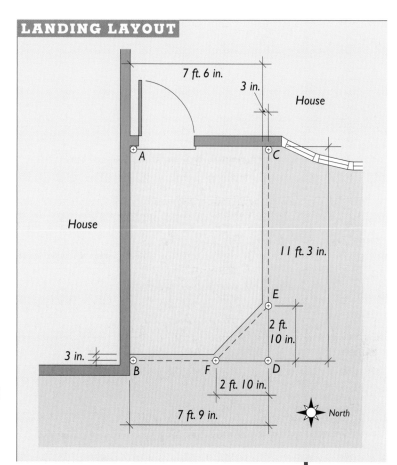

LANDING LAYOUT

7 ft. 6 in.

3 in.

House

A

C

House

11 ft. 3 in.

E

2 ft. 10 in.

3 in.

B   F   D

2 ft. 10 in.

7 ft. 9 in.

North

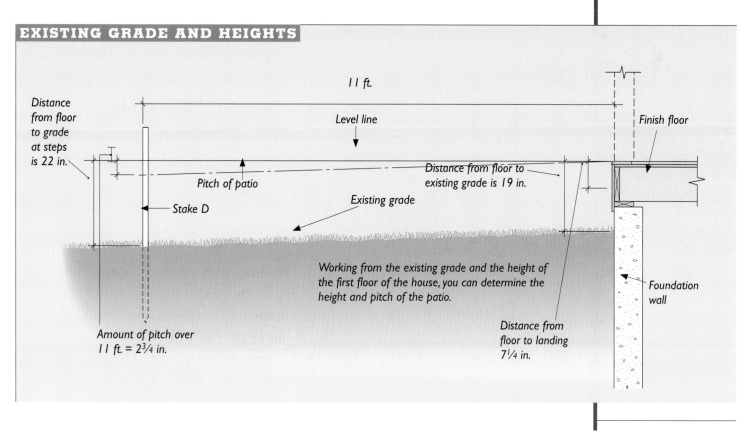

EXISTING GRADE AND HEIGHTS

11 ft.

Distance from floor to grade at steps is 22 in.

Level line

Finish floor

Pitch of patio

Distance from floor to existing grade is 19 in.

Stake D

Existing grade

Working from the existing grade and the height of the first floor of the house, you can determine the height and pitch of the patio.

Amount of pitch over 11 ft. = 2¾ in.

Distance from floor to landing 7¼ in.

Foundation wall

dimension equals the height of the riser at the front door.

4. The concrete wall blocks used for this project are 6 in. thick, 16 in. long, and 12 in. deep, and the wall cap is 3 in. thick. Given that the distance from the top of the walkway to the landing is 12 in. (the height of two risers) and that a portion of the first course of block is installed below grade, two courses of wall block plus the cap are needed to construct the retaining wall.

Initial walkway layout

After locating and determining the height of the landing, do the initial layout of the walkway.

1. Mark the beginning of the new walkway. First, measure to and mark one side of the walkway (18 ft. 6 in. from the garage for this project). You can install a stake or indicate the location with marking paint. Then measure and mark the width of the walkway entrance. Although this walkway is 4 ft. wide, it curves out to 8 ft. wide at the entrance (see the bottom drawing on p. 126).

2. From stakes E and F to the landing steps, arrange a hose or two to the shape and width of the walkway **A**. With marking paint, make a series of dots along the hoses, remove the hoses, and paint two lines by connecting the dots. This is the outline of the walkway.

3. To provide proper support for the concrete pavers, the base should be about 6 in. wider than the walkway on each side. Make a series of dots 6 in. from the walkway lines and paint two additional lines. These lines represent the base **B**. You can also mark out the location of new planting beds adjacent to the walkway.

Excavate the Walk and Demolish the Steps

After the initial layout, excavate the walkway and landing area. This project required the demolition of the existing asphalt walkway and concrete stoop.

1. Excavate the width and length of the walkway to the proper depth. The depth of excavation varies with soil type and climate (see p. 34). In this case, about 12 in. was removed. Although it is certainly possible to dig out the base by hand, you might find it a good investment to

the pieces of concrete that will be buried underneath the landing and rake it smooth .

2. Using a mechanical plate compactor, thoroughly compact the base material **B**. If it takes more than the recommended 3-in. to 4-in. lifts to cover the demolished pieces of concrete, take extra time to compact this area. In addition, run the compactor along the excavated walkway to compact any subsoil that might have been loosened during excavation.

hire an excavating contractor to do the work, or rent a piece of equipment and do it yourself.

2. Demolish the existing set of steps **A**. It's usually best to start at the end or the edge of the bottom step and work your way methodically up from there. Be sure to wear eye protection, and keep people a safe distance away so they won't get hit with flying pieces of concrete.

Install the Base

A crushed, recycled material was used as a base for this project. Because the area around the new steps required a significant amount of fill, the base was partially completed before the final layout for the steps and walkway was done. We used the broken-up concrete steps as part of the fill. If you like, you can do the final layout first and then install the landing base. (For more information on installing a base, see p. 37).

1. Using the marks you made on the foundation during the initial layout as a guide, begin to fill the landing area with base material. Because the base should extend beyond the width of the landing, spread the base material 6 in. past the marks on the foundation. Cover

(For more information on installing a base, see p. 37).

WHAT CAN GO WRONG

To save landfill space and money, demolition material can be used as fill underneath the new entry landing. However, before burying demolition material, check with your local building inspector and/or health agent to make sure that the practice is allowed. Generally, burying such material on private property is not allowed unless the material is used as construction fill.

WHAT CAN GO WRONG

Demolition can bring surprises. If, as you begin breaking away the steps, you discover that they are cast-in-place, which tend to be thicker than precast steps, it can be slow going. You can still demolish the steps by hand, but the thick concrete makes the job tougher and usually requires an electric jackhammer, which you can rent, to break it up.

3. Place 3-in. to 4-in. lifts of base material in the walkway excavation, rake it smooth, and compact it. When hand-tamping in areas where the plate compactor can't reach, such as in corners or along walls, tamp smaller lifts of about 2 in.

Establish the Final Heights and Layout

Utilizing the information gathered in the initial layout step on p. 126, establish the final heights and layout for the steps and landing.

1. Measure down from the first floor the distance to the top of the landing, and make a mark on the foundation or box sill, 7¼ in. for this project **A**.

2. Install stake A in the corner of the building. Level over from the top-of-landing mark you just made, and mark this stake **B**.

3. Measure approximately 3 in. out from the length and width marks on the foundation and install two stakes, B and C (see the top drawing on p. 127). These stakes are set outside the perimeter of the wall so that they won't be in the way as the retaining wall is constructed. Then tie a string to stake A at the top-of-landing mark, and using a line level, transfer this mark to stakes B and C. These marks are level with the top-of-landing mark **C**.

4. Establish the location of the stairs, which is at 45 degrees to the retaining wall (see the sidebar at right). First, pull one measuring tape from stake B and one from stake C the correct distance, 7 ft. 9 in. and 11 ft. 3 in., respectively.

D

E

Finding a Right Angle

TO LAY OUT A CORNER OR A SET OF STEPS at a 45-degree angle, you must do a simple mathematic calculation. Remember the Pythagorean theorem from math class? To paraphrase, it says that in a right triangle (one with a 90-degree angle) the length of the hypotenuse is equal to the sum of the squares of the other two sides or $A^2 + B^2 = C^2$, where C^2 is the hypotenuse. To lay out a 45-degree corner of a specific length, you work backward from C to calculate the length of the other two sides, which are equal. This requires the use of "cosines," but don't panic. You can simply multiply by 0.71. For example, for a 4-ft.-long 45-degree corner, you would do this math problem: 4 ft. x 0.71 = 2 ft. $10^{1/6}$ in. So the length of each of the sides is 2 ft. $10^{1/16}$ in., which can be rounded down to 2 ft. 10 in.

45-Degree Layout
To determine where to locate a 45-degree corner to create a specific length for the hypotenuse, first multiply the desired length by the factor 0.71. Then measure in from the corner the calculated distance. The resulting hypotenuse will be the desired length.

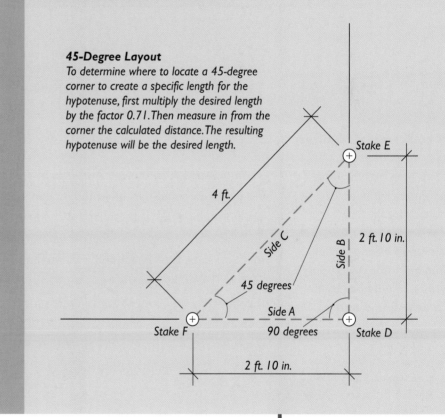

Install stake D where they intersect **D**. Measure down from the level mark on stake B the amount of pitch ($2^3/4$ in. here), level over to D, and mark the top of the landing. Pull a string at the level marks on stake B around stake D and on to stake C.

5. To locate the front of the second riser, measure back along the strings from stake D the correct distance and install stakes E and F **E**.

6. Determine the height of the landing (which is the same as the top tread), the first tread, and the walkway. From where the string crosses stake E, measure down the amount that the landing pitches to this point, 2 in. (11 ft. – 2 ft. 10 in. x $^1/4$ in. per ft.) for this project. From this mark, level over to and mark stake F. Because

the two sides of this landing are not equal, the shorter side pitches slightly more from stakes E to F than the other side. (For a square landing or patio, the pitches will be the same.) From the top-of-landing marks on stakes E and F, measure down the distance to the top of the first step and the top of walkway. Then, from the top-of-walkway mark, measure down the dis-

PROTIP

If your project requires many calculations, save time and increase accuracy by using a calculator that adds, subtracts, multiplies, and divides feet and inches. Lumberyards and supply yards usually sell them, as do online catalogs.

TRADE SECRET

As a general rule, at least 10 percent of the above-grade height of a concrete block wall should be underground. For example, a 24-in.-high wall should have 2½ in. underground.

tance to the top of the base . The pavers used for this project are 2⅜ in. thick and installed on a 1-in. setting bed. When they are compacted, the pavers will settle about ⅜ in., which means the top of the base must be 3 in. below the top of the walkway.

7. Before beginning to build the retaining wall, finish installing the walkway base. When you're done, attach a string at the top-of-walkway mark on stake E or F and pull it to the beginning of the walkway, securing it at the top of the driveway. To be sure you have the proper base depth along the whole walkway, at regular intervals measure the distance from the string to the base and adjust as needed .

Build the Landing

Building a raised landing requires the construction of a retaining wall. As determined in "Initial Walkway Layout" (p. 128), the wall for this project is two courses high plus a wall cap. The wall blocks are 6 in. thick, 16 in. long, and 12 in. wide, and the cap is 3 in. thick.

Complete the wall base

Although much of the wall base was installed earlier in conjunction with the walkway base, it needs to be completed before building the wall. The first task is to set the height of the top of the wall base and first course of wall block.

1. At stakes C and E, measure down from the top-of-landing mark the distance to the top of the first course of wall block, which is 9 in. for this project (6-in. block + 3-in. cap), and tie a string between them. This indicates the top of the first course of block.

2. Measure down to the base and continue to fill with additional base material. Fill until the base is approximately the thickness of a wall block plus 1 in. below the string, or 7 in. for this project.

3. Lay geotextile fabric over the base and cover it with about 1½ in. of base material. Later, you'll wrap the fabric up the sides of the block to keep soil and sand from infiltrating the gravel drainage material placed behind the wall.

Build the retaining wall

Once the base prep is completed, you can start to build the wall. When building a wall that meets at a 45-degree set of steps, it's best to start at the two ends and work toward the steps.

1. Position a full-length block at one end of the wall, aligning it with the mark on the wall. Set it into place by hitting it with a heavy rubber mallet or a small sledgehammer. Cushion the sledgehammer blow with a short piece of 2x4 to protect the block **A**. To maintain the proper pitch, the top edge of the block should be aligned lengthwise with the string.

2. Check the block to make sure it is level front to back **B**. Adjust as necessary by either adding or taking material away from under the block.

3. When the first block is installed, place a second block next to it and position it in a similar

manner **C**. Keep in mind that because the landing slopes, the wall blocks have to follow the same pitch, which is indicated by the string.

4. You can continue laying blocks until you reach stakes E and F, or, as we did for this project, you can begin the second course after laying two or three first-course blocks. Keep the face of the first course straight by checking it with a long straightedge and verify that it is running square to the building. Because

WHAT CAN GO WRONG

Installing a raised landing against the sides of a house can trap water and moisture, creating conditions that lead to rot. To avoid this potential problem, remove any wood siding that will be covered by the landing and install metal flashing (see also the drawing on p. 33). The house for this project is sided with vinyl, which extends below the wood framing and covers the foundation. A membrane flashing was installed behind the siding as a precaution.

guide strings can sometimes get knocked out of alignment, it's best to use the 3-4-5 triangle to check for square (see p. 40).

If you decide to start the second course before completing the bottom course, move the string up to the top-of-landing marks or add a second string and leave the lower string in place. It is important to stagger the joints, so use a half-block to start the second course (if you're building more than two courses, you'll alternate like this for the rest of the courses). Wall blocks are typically made with a notch at the halfway point in the back to make it easier to cut them into half-blocks. First, score the top and bottom of a block using a hammer and chisel. Then turn the block on its face and score along the notch, continuing until the block breaks in two **D**.

5. Install the half-block. Some types of wall blocks utilize tongue-and-groove systems to lock the blocks together, while others use a pin-and-hole system. The wall blocks for this project use pins. Using the number of pins suggested by the manufacturer, install them in the

proper holes. To install a block, line up the holes with the pins and slide the block in place **E**. You might have to jiggle the block to get it to go down, but don't move the block below it.

6. Continue installing blocks in this manner until the walls are constructed a little beyond stakes E and F **F**.

7. Temporarily lay the cap blocks in place to make sure that their tops align with the string set at the top-of-landing mark **G**. After the steps have been installed, the caps will be removed and then glued in their final position.

Build the steps

For this project, we used precast, single-piece riser/tread combinations. One-piece steps can either be cut "into" the landing or constructed separately. This project uses the cut-in approach, with steps that are 4 ft. wide, 6 in. thick (or high), and 1 ft. 3 in. deep (see the drawing at right). For information on how to construct steps separately, see the sidebar on p. 136.

Locate the first step The first stair-building task is to locate the position of the front of the first step, which is similar to the layout step above.

1. Remove stakes D, E, and F. Locate the position for stake G. Pull a string along the face of

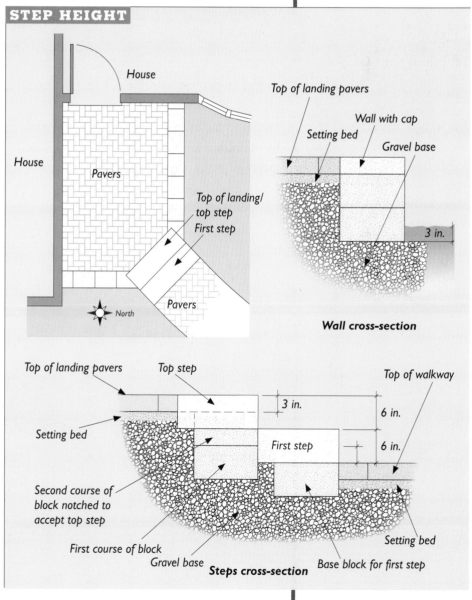

STEP HEIGHT

House

Pavers

North

House

Pavers

Top of landing/
top step

First step

Top of landing pavers

Setting bed

Wall with cap

Gravel base

3 in.

Wall cross-section

Top of landing pavers

Top step

Setting bed

Second course of block notched to accept top step

First step

3 in.

6 in.

6 in.

Top of walkway

First course of block

Gravel base

Base block for first step

Setting bed

Steps cross-section

Alternate Step Design

INSTEAD OF CUTTING ONE-PIECE STEPS INTO A LANDING WALL, it's also possible to complete the wall and then add the steps in front of the wall face. For example, in this project the 45-degree angle section of the wall would be finished and made 4 ft. wide to match the width of the stair tread. The base would have butted up against the wall and projected out 1 ft. 3 in. to support the tread, which is placed on top of the base. With this type of construction, the wall cap acts as the top tread. (For more on building steps, see p. 51.)

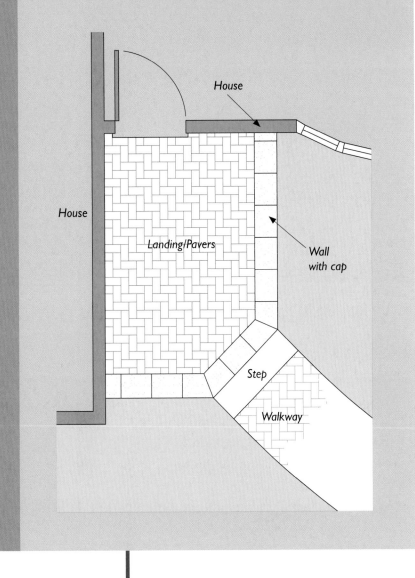

each wall and install stake G where they cross (see the left drawing on the facing page).

2. To locate the ends of the steps, measure back the correct distance along each string from stake G—2 ft. 10 in. for these 4-ft.-wide steps—and mark the edges of the partially completed wall. Then draw a line or pull a string between these marks (see the left drawing on the facing page).

3. The back of the top tread will be 9 in. in from the face of the wall/top cap. From the diagonal line you just marked in step 2, measure back 9 in. using a square, and draw another line to represent the back of the top tread (see the right drawing on the facing page).

4. From the back of the top tread, measure the total run of the two steps, 2 ft. 6 in. in this example (2 steps × 1 ft. 3 in. tread depth). Mark this location on the ground to position the front of the first step.

Install the first step After you've marked its location, install the first step. The stair base has to be installed first. Because the concrete paver walkway butts into the steps, the base needs to incorporate something solid in addition to compacted gravel. This keeps the gravel from migrating out from under the first step, which would cause the step to tip downward. Wall blocks are used as the base here.

1. Remove the blocks in the second course of the wall that intersect the top tread. These will be cut and replaced after the first step is installed.

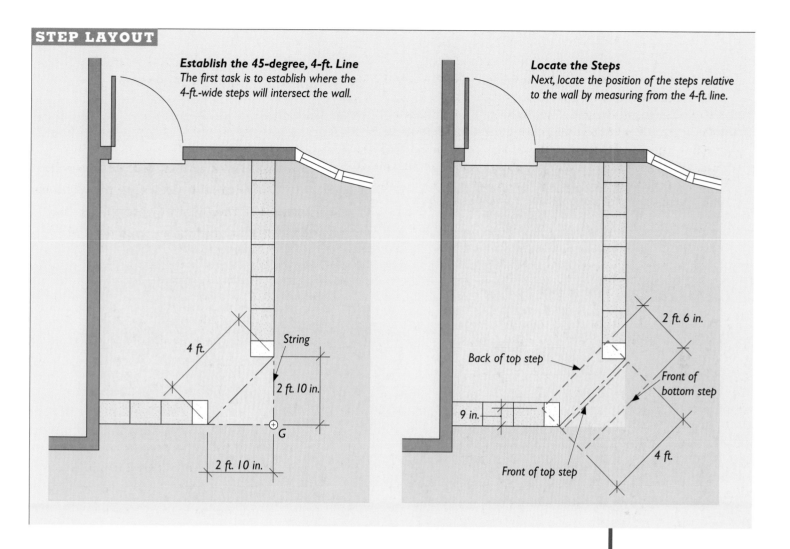

Establish the 45-degree, 4-ft. Line
The first task is to establish where the 4-ft.-wide steps will intersect the wall.

4 ft.

String

2 ft. 10 in.

G

2 ft. 10 in.

Locate the Steps
Next, locate the position of the steps relative to the wall by measuring from the 4-ft. line.

2 ft. 6 in.

Back of top step

Front of bottom step

9 in.

Front of top step

4 ft.

2. Because the top step will be flush with the 3-in.-thick cap, the step and the wall courses do not align. The bottom of the first step is 12 in. below the top of the landing (see the drawing on p. 135). Arrange the wall blocks for the stair base on top of the gravel base so that the blocks are the width of the steps aligned with the location of the front of the step **H**. Level the blocks front to back and across, and make sure they are 3 in. lower than the top of the bottom course of block. Because the wall blocks angle in front to back, to keep the base square the end blocks have to be cut and filled in with larger triangular pieces.

3. Position the first step in front of the base, and lift it on top of the base. Slide it into its final position with the help of a pry bar **I**. Check to make sure the step is level in both directions and is the proper distance from the 9-in. mark on the wall, 2 ft. 6 in. in this case.

Cut the wall block Before the top step can be installed, the second course of wall block has to be cut.

1. Replace the second-course blocks that were temporarily removed. They may have to be shortened to fit next to the first step. Position

PROTIP

When working alone, slip a small-diameter nail into one of the joints between the wall blocks and use it to hold the string.

PROTIP

Depending on the depth of the cut, when using a circular saw to cut block, it may be easier to make more than one pass, cutting deeper with each successive pass.

the 18-in. blade of a framing square along the outside of the front edge of the first tread. Draw a line along the 30-in. blade **J**. This line represents one side of the top tread.

2. Place the square on top of the first tread, and mark the front and side of the block to indicate the depth of the cut **K**.

3. Extend the top line to the end of the block, and make a vertical mark on the face of the wall block **L**.

4. After all the marks are made, cut out the piece of block. A circular saw equipped with a diamond blade can be used, but a cut-off saw is faster **M**.

5. Mark and cut the block on the other side of the step, then reposition the cut wall blocks. Using a 4-ft. level, make sure that the cuts are level across the width and with the top of the first step **N**. Carefully remove any excess material as needed to make the cuts smooth **O**.

Install the top step and cap After the cuts are done and wall blocks positioned, install the top step.

1. Move the top step into position and lift it onto the cut blocks. This is easier to do with a helper **P**.

2. Check that this step is positioned properly relative to the first step and is aligned with the top of the wall **Q**.

3. Cut and fit the cap pieces. Temporarily lay each cap in place, and mark the location of the cuts on the bottom of the cap **R**. Cut the cap pieces. Test-fit the caps and adjust if necessary **S**.

4. Before permanently installing the caps, finish backfilling the landing area. Place washed stone in between the wall and the geotextile fabric to just below the bottom of the cap **T**.

Fold the fabric over the top of the wall. Add base material to the whole landing area, wet it as needed , and compact it. The base should be 3 in. below the top of the wall, which is enough space to accommodate the setting bed and pavers.

5. Remove all the caps, and turn them upside down to avoid getting the bottoms dirty. Apply adhesive to the top of the wall according to the manufacturer's recommendations . Put the caps back on the top of the wall. Use a level to make sure they are aligned , then tap them in place with a rubber mallet or small sledgehammer cushioned by a block of wood.

WHAT CAN GO WRONG

Applying adhesives can be a messy activity. To clean up your tools and hands, be sure to have the proper cleaning solvent on hand before you begin to work.

Install the Landing Pavers

With the wall and steps completed, install the concrete pavers in the landing. For more detailed information on installing concrete pavers, refer to p. 41 and p. 83.

Install the setting bed

A carefully and accurately prepared setting bed is a crucial part of working successfully with pavers. Concrete paver manufacturers recommend using concrete sand, which is coarser than other sands. The setting bed should be 1 in. thick, so you'll use 1-in. pipes to get the measurement right. This project is small enough so that the entire setting bed can be covered with pavers in one working session. If your project is larger and the setting bed too big to finish in one session, install only as much setting bed as you can cover with pavers before you stop work for the day.

1. Make sure that the base is at the proper height and pitches properly. The pavers used for this project are $2\frac{3}{8}$ in. thick and will settle about $\frac{3}{8}$ in. when they are compacted. This means that the base should be 3 in. below the top of the wall caps—$\frac{5}{8}$ in. for the compacted sand bed and $2\frac{3}{8}$ in. for the pavers.

2. Lay two 1-in. pipes on top of the base, spaced about 3 ft. apart. Put a level along the length of the pipes to make sure that they maintain the $\frac{1}{4}$-in.-per-ft. pitch and from pipe to pipe to make sure they are level with each other. Adjust the pipes as necessary. To make sure that the pavers and cap are properly aligned, place a paver on top of the pipes and hold it up against the cap **A**. It should be $\frac{3}{8}$ in. above it

3. Shovel sand on top of the base, first at the ends of the pipes to hold them in place and then enough to cover the pipes. Fill the area around the pipes, and rake it out. Screed the surface. Repeat this process until the entire setting bed has been completed.

4. When you've finished screeding the setting bed, carefully remove the pipes **B**. Using

a trowel and additional sand, fill the voids and smooth them. If you can't reach a void from outside of the setting bed, wait to fill it in until after you've installed some pavers.

Lay the pavers

The pavers for this landing are laid in a 90-degree herringbone pattern. Because the landing is relatively small, the pattern was begun at a corner against the house wall. For larger projects, it's better to start at the middle and work toward the ends.

1. Begin the pattern by laying one paver perpendicular to the landing wall. Lay the second one parallel to the wall, butting against the first paver. Repeat this pattern, nesting the next two pavers into the first two

2. Continue laying pavers in this manner. At regular intervals, you will end up with an open space or hole that's the size of one-half a paver **D**. Just leave it open, and keep installing pavers around it. It's much more efficient to leave the spaces open for now and cut half-sized pavers to fit at the end, all at once. Once

you need to kneel on the pavers to continue the installation, kneel on a piece of plywood instead of the pavers themselves so that you don't compress individual pavers.

3. When all the full-size pavers are installed, measure, cut, and install the half-size pavers. You can measure with a tape measure **E** or by placing each paver next to a hole and marking the length directly on the paver. The larger

PRO**TIP**

To make sure that the open spaces along the edges of a pattern don't get squeezed in or opened up, use a short piece of full-width paver as a spacer to test each opening.

pieces can be cut with a guillotine cutter **F** and the smaller ones with a saw.

4. Slide each cut paver into place. Tap it with a rubber mallet if necessary to bring it flush with the neighboring pavers **G**.

Compact the pavers and fill the joints

Edge restraints are not necessary because the wall caps act as edge restraints, so you can go ahead and compact the pavers now.

1. Spread a thin layer of concrete sand over the top of the pavers. The sand will protect the pavers as they are compacted, and a small amount will find its way into each joint, helping to lock the pavers in place.

2. Using a mechanical plate compactor, compact the pavers until they are flush with the top of the wall caps **H**. As you compact the pavers next to the cap, tip the compactor back slightly so it doesn't sit fully on the cap and chip it. Remove any excess concrete sand.

3. Lastly, fill the joints with polymeric sand. Following the manufacturer's directions, spread some polymeric sand over the stones and sweep it into the joints until they are filled to the top **I**. Remove excess sand, and beginning at the higher area near the house, wet the pavers and joints with a light spray of water. Let it cure completely before walking on it.

Complete the Walkway

All that remains now is to complete the walkway. That means doing the final layout and installing the walkway pavers. Again, for more detailed information, refer to pp. 39–44 and pp. 81–91.

Do the final layout

1. Make sure that the base is at the proper height, which is 3 in. below the bottom of the first step and the top of the driveway.

2. Using a hose, lay out the final shape of the walkway, and paint the outline on both sides of the walkway.

3. Install pin flags at regular intervals along both lines to mark the edge of the walkway **A**.

Install the setting bed

1. Beginning at the landing steps, lay two 1-in. pipes about 3 ft. apart. Use a level to check the cross-pitch—¼ in. per ft., or 1 in. over the 4-ft. width of this walkway.

2. Fill the area with concrete sand and screed it.

3. Repeat this process until the entire setting bed is done. If you will not be able to lay all the pavers during one work session, only install as much setting bed as you can cover in one session.

Install the pavers

The pavers for this landing are laid in a 45-degree herringbone pattern. In this project, the pavers are aligned with their joints turned 45 degrees to the face of the landing steps.

1. To establish the 45-degree angle, pull a string parallel to the face of the first step, tying it to two stakes. Measuring from the intersection of the two strings and using the 3-4-5 triangle method (see the drawing on p. 40), pull another string at a 45-degree angle to the first and secure it to two stakes **B**.

2. Install the first paver with its end against the string and about one paver-length away from the step **C**. Leaving a space there allows room for discrepancies.

3. Add a few more pavers, building the pattern as you did for the landing on p.143, and then move to the other side of the line. Continue working near the steps until you've covered the setting bed that's underneath the string **D**.

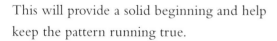

This will provide a solid beginning and help keep the pattern running true.

4. Kneeling on a piece of plywood, continue laying pavers along the length of the path **E**. Be sure to extend some of the pavers beyond the finished edge of the walkway, which is indicated by the pin flags.

Cut the pavers and install the edge restraints

Because they define the finished walkway edge, the edge restraints are installed after the last pavers are cut and put in place.

1. To outline the walkway's finished edge, place edge restraints along one side of the walk and, using the pin flags as a guide, bend them into the proper shape **F**. You can hold the restraints in place with some pavers.

2. Using the edge restraint as a guide, score a line with a cut-off saw **G**. You can also mark the cutline with a marking crayon.

3. Carefully remove each paver that has a cut mark, and cut it using a cut-off saw. While cutting, hold the paver down with a 2x4 **H**.

4. Fill in the remaining pieces by placing pavers, or scrap pieces of pavers, in the empty spaces, marking them, and cutting them to the

right size. Continue until all the pavers on this side of the walkway are done.

5. Install the edge restraints along this side of the walkway. Make sure that the restraints are held securely up against the edge of the pavers as you install them .

6. Repeat steps 1 through 5 for the other side of the walkway.

Compact the pavers and fill the joints

After the edge restraints have been installed on both sides of the walkway, compact the pavers and fill in the joints (see p. 144 for instructions).

MAKE A BOLD ENTRANCE

Garages, rather than the home's front entrance, often dominate the approach to a house. And while homeowners may enter their homes through the garage, guests are often left standing in the driveway trying to figure out where to go. This problem is made worse when there are two walkways off the driveway.

The solution is multi-faceted. First, clearly differentiate between the choices, and make the approach to the front door prominent and obvious. Then, because the distance to the front door from the garage can be long, design a walkway that escorts your guests in style. Finally, create a sense of transition and arrival with broad steps and a sumptuous landing. ▶ ▶ ▶

Layouts and Heights

When a project consists of two or more parts—for example, an entry patio, stairs, and a walkway—it often makes sense to divide the layout and construction into phases. This is particularly true when access to the site is limited and materials need to be transported over one area or another.

Raising the grade next to a house requires the construction of retaining walls. For this project, plans call for stone retaining walls to raise the grade on both sides of the front door. These walls are built in conjunction with two sets of steps. The initial task is to lay out the overall length and width of the new stone entry patio and stone walls.

Lay out and build the northern retaining wall

1. Lay out the retaining wall to the north of the front door. Install a stake, A, 16 ft. away from, and in line with, the northwest corner of the house. Then, running parallel to the house, install stake B 31 ft. 6 in. from stake A. Stake A marks the outside of the wall and stake B the location of the first step up to the entry patio (see the drawing on p. 154).

2. Lay out the 6-ft. radius section of the wall. Measure 6 ft. in from the corner of the foundation and 10 ft. out from the corner, and install a radius stake R1 (see the drawing on p. 154).

3. Set the tape at the radius distance, 6 ft., and swing an arc. You can install stakes along this arc and paint a line later, or paint a line as you swing the arc.

4. The new grade adjacent to the house foundation is 1 ft. 6 in. below the first floor. This is

Prepare the Site

When plans call for extensive changes around an existing house, site preparation typically begins with the removal of all the plantings in the work area. Tag all those that are to be saved and pot them or temporarily install them somewhere else on your property.

Demolition takes place next. A stoop and walkway can typically be removed with hand tools, as shown in **A**. (For information on demolishing concrete walkways, see p. 110).

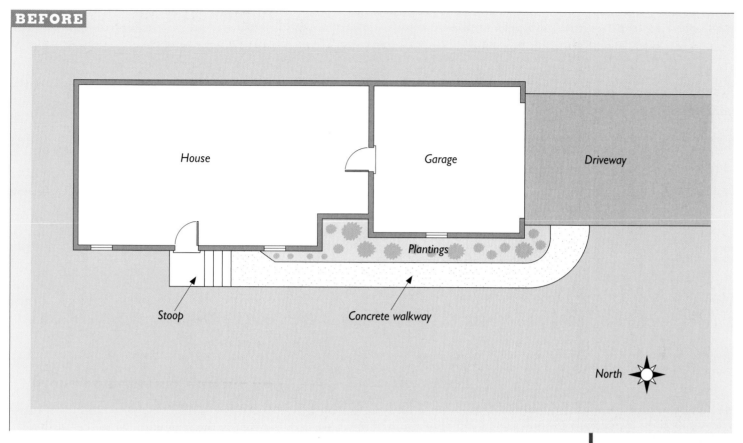

House

Garage

Driveway

Plantings

Stoop

Concrete walkway

North

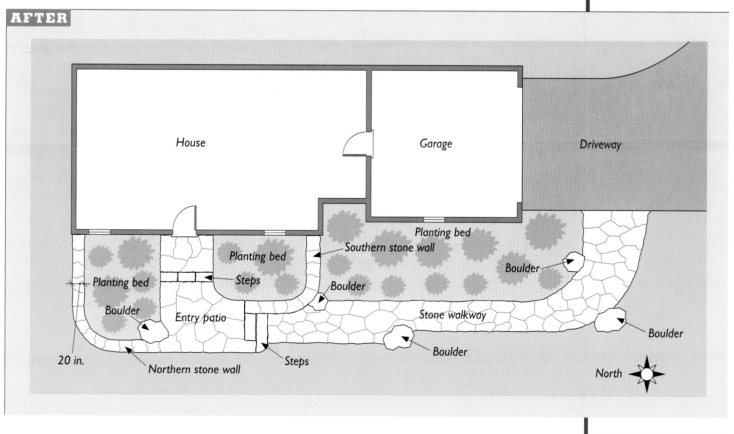

House

Garage

Driveway

Planting bed

Southern stone wall

Planting bed

Steps

Boulder

Boulder

Planting bed

Boulder

Entry patio

Stone walkway

Boulder

20 in.

Northern stone wall

Steps

Boulder

North

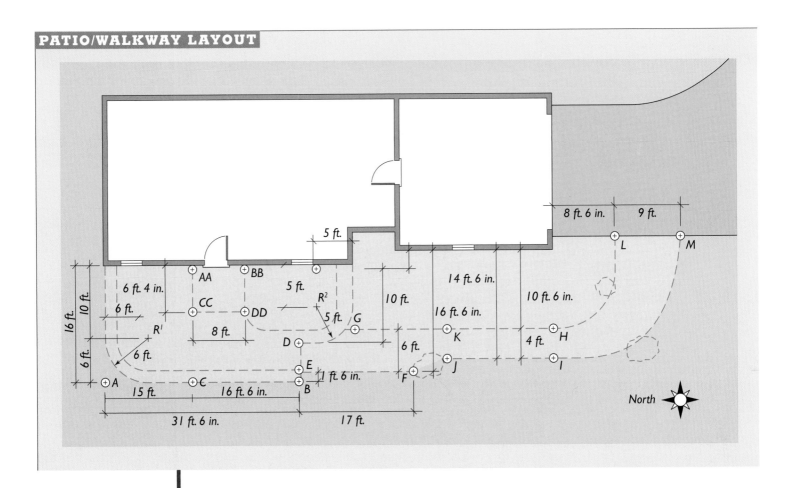

the same height as the portion of the retaining wall that abuts the house. However, because the entry patio slopes away from the house, the wall is about 2 in. lower at the outside edge of the patio than it is next to the house (see "Build the Entry Patio" on p. 158). At the corner of the foundation mark 1 ft. 6 in. below the first floor, pull a string with a line level on it to stake A and make a mark. Measure down 2 in. and make another mark. From the mark you just made, pull a string level to stake B and mark this stake. This string represents the top of the wall and patio.

5. On stake B, mark the height of the existing grade, which, in this project, is the top of the walkway.

6. Before the location of the new front door steps can be determined, the stone wall must be constructed and the surrounding grade raised to the desired height. For this project, the wall was constructed to approximately 3 ft. short of stake B, where the patio steps begin, and completed as the steps were built. (For information on building stone walls, see p. 44.) Install the base material, lay geotextile fabric on top of the base, and, as the wall is built, fill the area directly behind the washed or crushed stone and the planting bed area with subsoil and then loam. Fill the area underneath the steps and patio with a base material. We used a material known locally as trap-rock screenings, which is finer than crushed stone or gravel. (For information on installing a base, see p. 37.)

Lay out the front door steps

Once the grade below the front door is brought to the proper height, lay out the front steps.

1. From the center of the door, measure one half the width of the steps to either side and make a mark .

2. Plumb down from these marks with a level and install stakes—AA, BB—at each location (see the drawing on the facing page).

3. Mark the heights of the steps and base on the stakes. For this project, the finish grade, which is the same as the top of the patio, is 1 ft. 6 in. below the first floor. This means that three 6-in. risers are required to reach the first floor. To find their locations, measure down from the first floor 6 in. and mark that measurement

A

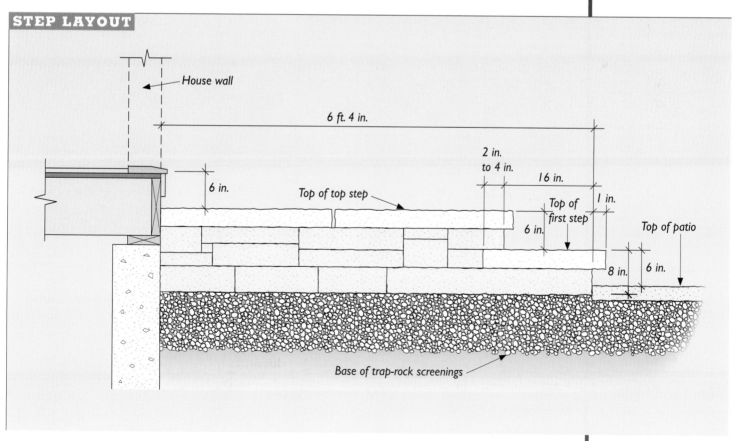

STEP LAYOUT

House wall

6 ft. 4 in.

6 in.

Top of top step

2 in. to 4 in.

16 in.

Top of first step

1 in.

6 in.

Top of patio

8 in.

6 in.

Base of trap-rock screenings

B

C

D

PRO TIP

An easy way to get a measurement that's approximately perpendicular to a building is to use a framing square to guide the tape measure.

PRO TIP

If a level isn't long enough to do the job— try holding two levels together. You may need two people for this job.

on the stakes. This represents the top of the top step. From this mark, measure down another 6 in. to mark the top of the first step.

4. To get locked into place, the bottom of the first riser sits on top of the stair base, which is located about 2 in. below the top of the patio (see the drawing on p. 155). From the mark for the first step, measure down 8 in. and mark the stakes **B**.

5. Lay out the depth of the steps. From stake AA and from BB, measure out perpendicularly from the wall the distance to the front of the first step (6 ft. 4 in. in this example) and install stakes CC and DD, respectively (see the drawing on p. 154). To make sure the stakes are square, measure the diagonals **C**. The two distances should be equal. If they aren't, move the stakes as necessary until the measurements are equal and the stakes are square to the foundation.

6. Using a level or a line level, transfer the stair and base heights to these two stakes **D**.

7. Next, locate the north edge of the entry patio, which is in line with the steps. Install a stake (C) in line with stakes B and CC/AA (see the drawing on p. 154).

8. When the stair layout is complete, add additional material to bring the base up to the base mark, and compact thoroughly.

Moving Large Stones

MOVING LARGE, HEAVY STONES might seem like an overwhelming challenge, but with a little leverage and some patience, you'll be able to move even the largest stone. You need three tools: wooden blocks, rollers, and a large pry bar. Sturdy wooden planks can also come in handy.

To start, position a block at one end of the stone and wedge the pry bar under the stone, above the block. Push down on the bar to lift the stone, and have a helper slide a roller under the width of the stone about one-third the length in from the end. If you are working alone, position the roller next to the block, and as you lift the stone, push it underneath with your foot. You may have to pry and block the stone a couple of times before the roller will fit under it. Move to the other end of the stone and repeat this process.

With the stone supported on the rollers, place a third roller at the end of the stone in the direction that you want to move the stone. Move to the other end of the stone, place the pry bar under the stone, and lift it, pushing against the stone. The rollers should rotate, moving the stone forward. If the rollers dig into the base material and don't rotate, you can put the rollers on planks.

As you push the stone, it will move forward onto the top of the third roller and off the first roller. Move the first roller to the other end of the stone and continue to push. This task is easier if the stone is always supported by at least two rollers.

When you reach the final destination, you can use the block and pry bar to remove the rollers. If you need to lift the stone, as you would a tread to the top of a riser, leave the stone on the rollers. Depending on how high the stone has to go, you may be able to lift it into place with a pry bar, first lifting one, then the other end. To lift it higher, you can go up in stages, blocking up one end then the other until the stone is high enough to lift into place. You can also use two planks, each with one end resting on the ground and the other on top of the final location. Using a pry bar, inch one end and then the other up the planks.

Construct the Front Door Steps

Once the base for the stairs is finished, construct the front steps. The treads for these steps are made up of several stones, all about 3 in. thick. Having stones all the same thickness makes installation a lot easier.

1. At the base mark, fasten a string to the stakes around the perimeter of the stairs. This string also indicates the top of the base for patio stones. At the front two stakes, CC and DD, measure down from the first step mark 3 in., make a mark, and tie another string between the two stakes. This string indicates the top of the first riser stones (3-in. tread + 3-in. riser = 6-in. rise).

PRO TIP

When building single-stone risers, it helps to choose stones that are a little thicker than necessary. To get the exact height, you can dig the stone into the base slightly.

A

B

C

2. Install the first riser and the bottom course, which extends on both sides of the riser back toward the house. The plans call for the treads to overhang the stair base, so install the base stones about 1 in. inside the strings. Use a level to verify that the stones are level across the front and front to back, and to check the alignment of the tops of the stones **A**.

3. When the first riser is complete, fill and compact the area behind the riser so that it is flush with the top of the riser. Scrap pieces of stone can be mixed with the base material.

4. Install the first tread. Choose stones that are deep enough to extend about 2 in. to 4 in.

underneath the face of the next riser. This means that to get 16 in. of exposed stone for the steps, you need to use stones that are 18 in. to 20 in. deep.

5. Build the second riser as you did the first in step 2 **B**. Fill in behind it, and install the top tread **C**.

Build the Entry Patio

After the front door steps are complete, build the entry patio. To minimize the amount of disturbance moving the large patio stones can cause, all but a few stones of the patio are installed before laying out the walkway, patio steps, and second stone wall.

1. To shed water, the entry patio pitches down from the front of the first step to the wall about 2 percent (¼ in. per ft.). (For more information on pitch, see p. 33.) At stake CC, pull a string from the top of the patio (6 in. below the first tread) and tie it to the top-of-wall mark on stake C. This string represents the edge and top of the patio.

2. Build the patio base up to the proper height. The patio stones for this project average about

2 in. thick, so the base is built 2 in. below this string. Install the base in lifts of 3 in. to 4 in., compacting each lift completely. (For more information on installing bases, see p. 37.)

3. Install the first patio stones at the edge, in line with the string . Where the patio intersects the stone wall, the patio stones become the wall capstones **B**. You can use a digging or long pry bar to push stones snugly into place. You can also use the butt end of a digging bar to jam base material underneath the edge of a stone to bring it to the proper pitch or make them level.

4. Working from the northern end toward the southern end, continue installing patio stones **C**. Stop short of the entry patio steps to leave enough room to install the top tread, which is actually part of the patio. (See p. 118 for more information on installing patio stone.)

Lay Out and Build the Southern Wall

The next step is to lay out and start building the southern stone wall and the steps leading up to the patio. When steps are integrated into stone walls, the walls and steps are constructed simultaneously.

1. This stone wall is 10 ft. from the house foundation and has a curved section with a 5-ft. radius. The first task is to locate the center of the radius. From the corner, measure in 5 ft. on the foundation wall and perpendicularly out 5 ft., and install stakes at these points. Pull two measuring tapes from each stake, and where they cross at 5 ft. install a stake, R2. This is the center of the radius as shown in  **A** on p. 160.

PRO**TIP**

To make a straight line at an edge, it's faster and more accurate to choose stones that project beyond the string and trim the stones in place.

A

B

C

2. Locate the outside of the wall by swinging a tape in a 5-ft. arc from the radius stake, installing stakes at regular intervals along the arc and painting a curved line **B**. You can also paint the line using the tape measure as a guide and skip installing the intermediate stakes.

PROTIP

When building a wall, taking the time to get the first course as level as possible makes it much easier to keep successive courses level.

2. Locate the outside of the wall by swinging a tape in a 5-ft. arc from the radius stake, installing stakes at regular intervals along the arc and painting a curved line **B**. You can also paint the line using the tape measure as a guide and skip installing the intermediate stakes.

3. Dig out the area for the base under the southern wall and the patio steps. This low wall is about 12 in. wide, so the base needs to be about 2 in. wider on both sides, or 16 in. wide. Because much of the existing soil was removed during the demolition process, this base only needs to be a few inches thick. Trap-rock screenings are used for the base material. Install the base for this stone wall and for the patio steps.

4. Once the base is prepared, build the wall **C**. (For more information on wall construction, see p. 44 and p. 116.)

Lay Out and Build the Patio Steps

The layout and construction of the patio steps, which are 4 ft. wide, are done in conjunction with completing the retaining walls. The process works like this: Install the first riser and tread, then build each wall over the ends of the tread. Install the next riser and tread, and again build the wall over them. Finally, build the third riser and install the top tread/patio stone on the last riser. This stone serves as a tread, patio stone, and a capstone for both walls. The treads for this project are 16 in. deep; the risers are 6 in.

1. At stake B, measure the total distance from the top of the patio/wall to the top-of-walkway mark (1 ft. 6 in. in this example). Divide this figure by three to get the rise of each individual step, and mark the location of the top of both steps on stake B. Then at the edge of the southern retaining wall and in line with stake B, install stake D (see the drawing on p. 154). Pull a line level from stake B to stake D, and mark stake D with the tread heights **A**.

2. To create the desired overhang, install the first riser 1 in. inside the string. Tie the riser into the walls by extending the riser's stones at either end of the riser into the wall. Make sure it's level. Check the thickness of the tread you have chosen for this step and build the riser to the proper height to accommodate the tread **B**.

3. When the riser is finished, install the first tread. The tread for this project is a single piece of stone, but you can use two pieces. On the west end, the tread extends to the end of the wall, and at the east end, it extends into the retaining wall.

4. To locate the second riser, measure in from the front of the first tread the depth of the tread (see the drawing on p. 155). At this spot, build the riser to the correct height. Install the second tread and make sure it's level **C**.

5. Build the third riser and install the top tread, which is actually part of the patio. Finish building both walls **D**, and install the capstones, which are level with the top tread/patio. Install the remaining patio stones.

6. When the patio stones have all been installed, sweep stone dust into the cracks (see p. 167).

A

B

TRADE SECRET

When treads are installed in conjunction with walls, they should be built into the walls, not just touch them. Extending treads into a wall physically and visually locks them into place, making them feel and look more secure. However, unless the design calls for the tread to project completely through a wall, it only has to be buried a few inches.

Lay Out the Walkway

When the stone walls and steps are completed, lay out the walkway. Like many walkways, the side of this walkway that is nearest the house runs parallel to the house and garage wall. However, the other side jogs in and incorporates a boulder—a feature you might consider.

1. Begin the layout at the patio steps. This walkway is aligned vertically with the second tread, which is 1 ft. 6 in. inside the face of the first stone wall. Install a stake, E, at this location. Then measure how far this stake is from the house, 14 ft. 6 in. in this example. Install a second stake, F, 17 ft. from E and 16 ft. 6 in. from the garage, which jogs back from the house 2 ft. This is the point at which the walkway jogs (see the drawing on p. 154).

C

PROTIP

Polymeric sand can be used to fill the joints instead of stone dust, and mortar mix can be used at the vulnerable edges.

D

2. Lay out the width of the walkway. In line with the outside of the southern wall, install a stake, G, 6 ft. from stakes E and F. Measure how far stake G is from the house wall, which is 8 ft. 6 in. in this example.

3. At the location where the inside of the curve starts (at the corner of the garage for this project), measure away from the garage wall the correct distance, 10 ft. 6 in. for this project, and install a stake, H.

4. To establish the width of this section of the walkway, measure out from the garage wall 14 ft. 6 in. (8 ft. 6 in. plus the 4-ft. width of the walkway) and install two stakes, I and J (see the drawing on p. 154).

5. Locate the beginning of the walkway by measuring the desired distance out from the garage and then the width of the walkway entrance—8 ft. 6 in. and 9 ft., respectively, here. Install stakes L and M (see the drawing on p. 154), then lay out the inside and outside curves of the walkway. You can use a hose to lay out the curves and paint the outline/edges (see p. 30 for more on using a hose for layout).

Establish the Height of the Walkway

After the walkway is laid out, establish the height, or top, of the walkway. This walkway conforms to the topography of the existing grade, which slopes up from the driveway to the curve at

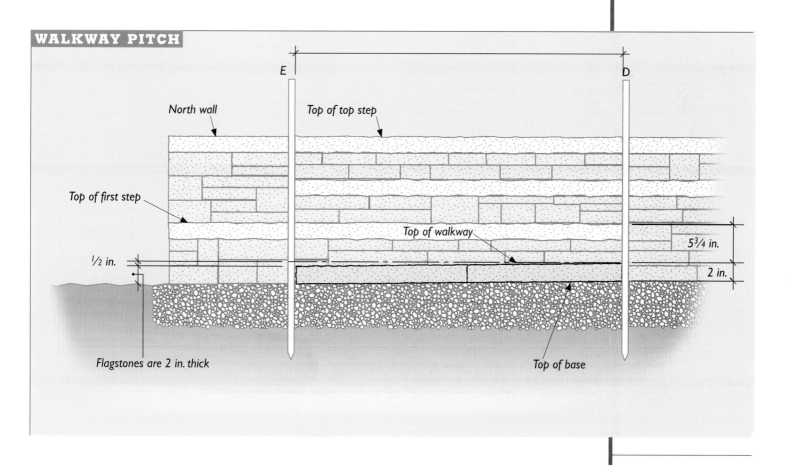

WALKWAY PITCH

North wall

Top of top step

Top of first step

Top of walkway

$5^3/4$ in.

2 in.

$^1/2$ in.

Top of base

Flagstones are 2 in. thick

E

D

stakes H and I and then slopes down to the patio steps. With the exception of the 6-ft.-wide section nearest the steps, this walkway does not have a cross-pitch.

1. To shed water near the patio steps, the walkway pitches ⅛ in. per ft. From the east end of the first entry patio step, measure down 5¾ in. and make a mark on stake D (see the drawing on p. 163). Using a line level or builder's site level, transfer this mark to stake E and measure down from this mark ½ in. These marks indicate the top of the walkway and the cross-pitch, respectively. Transfer the mark you just made on stake E to stake F.

2. Add stake K opposite stake J, where the width of the walkway changes. Locate the top of the existing grade at stakes G, H, I, and J, and mark them. Mark the top of the driveway on stakes L and M.

3. Tie strings to all the marks. The strings not only indicate the top of the walkway but also its width.

Excavate and Install the Base for the Walkway

After the walkway is laid out and the finished height established, excavate the outlined area. The exact depth varies with climate and soil type. Because the soil here drains well, the base was dug out about 8 in. below the finish grade to create a 6-in. base and allow for 2-in. stones. (For additional information on excavating, see p. 34.) Excavate 2 in. beyond each side of the strings, and compact the area with a hand tamper or plate compactor.

Install the base material, which is the same trap-rock screenings used for the patio. Because trap-rock screenings are finer and easier to manipulate than crushed gravel, they can be used for the base and, in lieu of stone dust, also as a setting bed. This means that the base and setting bed are combined **A**. To allow for the mica schist flagstone, which averages about 2 in., the top of the base is 2 in. below the strings.

Install Walkway Stones

After the base is installed, lay the walkway stones. Start laying the stones at the patio steps so you don't end up carrying stones over parts of the walkway you've already finished. (See p. 118 for more information on installing patio stone.) If you're installing boulders as design elements, install them before the walkway stones.

Incorporating Boulders

BOULDERS ARE EASY, NATURAL-LOOKING DESIGN ELEMENTS to add to your walkway. But boulders actually do much more than add an interesting visual element. They act as goals that pull people along, as markers of points of transition, and as anchors that help shape and define the walkway and patio.

Stones that are easily seen from the entrance invite people onto the walkway. Boulders can also mark transition points—where the walkway abruptly widens, for example, or at an intersection of retaining wall and steps.

A boulder's location on a front-entry patio like the one in this project encourages guests to climb the steps. A boulder can add mass to the corner of the patio, balancing the visual weight of the front door steps on one side.

1. If you will be installing any boulders along your walkway, do it before you lay any walkway stones. Measure the approximate diameter of each boulder. Dig a hole about 2 in. to 3 in. bigger than the boulder and deep enough to hold the boulder securely. Move the boulder into the hole, positioning it so that it sits "properly" in the hole and orienting it so that the face you like is visible from the walkway. Then fill in around the hole with soil.

2. Fit the first stones to the riser and along the south wall, following the pitch for this section.

3. As you work toward stakes F, J, and K, keep the patio aligned with the strings and use a level to make sure the tops of the walkway stones are aligned with each other. Fit the stones around the boulders see **A** on p. 166.

4. When you near stakes H and I, lay out the curve by eye. Install the stones in the curved section of the walkway. Stop when you get

A

B

C

D

near the beginning of the walkway. Install the entrance stone (or stones) that butt the driveway before completing the walkway, then fill in the remaining stones.

5. After the entrance stone is in place, measure the remaining spaces, and choose the largest possible stones to fill them in **B**.

6. Trim the edges of the previously installed walkway stones to approximate the shape of the stone you've chosen to install **C**. Position the stone over the space, supporting it on a couple

of 4x4s, with one 4x4 aligned with the edge of the stone below. Trim the top stone to fit. Repeat this at the other end **D**.

7. Using a pry bar, lift the stone, remove the 4×4s, and slowly lower the stone in place. If it doesn't fit, lift it and trim it some more until it does. Slide it into its final location with the pry bar and tamp it so that it is stable and aligned with the tops of the adjacent stones **E**.

8. Continue this process until you have completed the walkway **F**.

Fill the Joints

When all of the stones have been installed, fill the joints with stone dust. Spread a thin layer of the stone dust over the walkway and sweep it into the cracks. Remove the excess and wet the entire surface with a hose to compact it. Repeat as necessary until the cracks are completely filled. If you notice additional settling over time, install additional stone dust.

INDEX